CAREER
CROSSROADS

A HEADHUNTER'S GUIDE TO CAREER STRATEGY™

ADRIAN CHOO

Marshall Cavendish
Business

Published by Marshall Cavendish Business
An imprint of Marshall Cavendish International
1 New Industrial Road, Singapore 536196

Other Marshall Cavendish Offices:
Marshall Cavendish Corporation. 99 White Plains Road, Tarrytown NY 10591-9001,
USA • Marshall Cavendish International (Thailand) Co Ltd. 253 Asoke, 12th Flr,
Sukhumvit 21 Road, Klongtoey Nua, Wattana, Bangkok 10110, Thailand • Marshall
Cavendish (Malaysia) Sdn Bhd, Times Subang, Lot 46, Subang Hi-Tech Industrial Park,
Batu Tiga, 40000 Shah Alam, Selangor Darul Ehsan, Malaysia.

Marshall Cavendish is a trademark of Times Publishing Limited

National Library Board, Singapore Cataloguing-in-Publication Data
Choo, Adrian.
Career Crossroads : A headhunter's guide to career strategy / Adrian Choo. –
Singapore : Marshall Cavendish Business, [2015]
pages cm
ISBN : 978-981-4561-63-1

1. Career development. 2. Career changes. I. Title.

HF5381
650.14 — dc23   OCN899259827

Printed in Singapore by Fabulous Printers Pte Ltd

3930000556 3787

The Road Not Taken

Two roads diverged in a yellow wood,
And sorry I could not travel both
And be one traveler, long I stood
And looked down one as far as I could
To where it bent in the undergrowth;

Then took the other, as just as fair,
And having perhaps the better claim
Because it was grassy and wanted wear,
Though as for that the passing there
Had worn them really about the same,

And both that morning equally lay
In leaves no step had trodden black.
Oh, I kept the first for another day
Yet knowing how way leads on to way
I doubted if I should ever come back.

I shall be telling this with a sigh
Somewhere ages and ages hence:
Two roads diverged in a wood, and I,
I took the one less traveled by,
And that has made all the difference.

—ROBERT FROST (1874–1963)

Contents

Acknowledgements

This book would not have been possible without the help of family and friends. Firstly, I would like to thank my wife, Ping, for her unwavering support on this project, as well as my children Lucius and Mia, who despite their tender age, have cheered me on all the way.

I am thankful to my good friend, Low Wai Peng, for proofreading the document and making countless suggestions to improve it. I also appreciate the encouragement and wisdom of Andy Naylor and Maelyn Urquhart, the wonderful couple who took the time to critique my early manuscripts, and not forgetting Raymond Chee as well. Special mention goes to Lorraine Chin for her enthusiasm for the project. I also want to thank Khoo Swee Chiow the adventurer, for sharing his own Career Story with us and inspiring all of us to greater heights.

I would also like to thank my publisher, Marshall Cavendish, for their faith in my book, and especially to Mindy Pang, my editor who had to put up with my wanton abuse of the Oxford Comma.

I am blessed that along my career journey, I have met many mentors and friends who have helped me, especially my late mentor, Diana Young for being my greatest teacher and role model. A special thanks too, to my own career mentor, Bill Farrell from Taiwan for his superb advice.

Thanks and God Bless!

Introduction

It was a slow business day in the middle of the great financial crisis in 2008. Banks were on the verge of shutting down, the Dow Jones index was plummeting and the newspapers were awash with photographs of distressed traders.

Nobody was hiring. It had been a slow month for everyone. I was busy playing solitaire on my computer (business was *that* slow) when my phone suddenly rang.

The call was from Robert, a 46-year-old Information Technology (IT) manager in the manufacturing sector who had just received a retrenchment notice. He had been a loyal employee at his company for the past thirteen years and had recently paid a deposit for a million-dollar sea-facing condominium purchased at a 'fire-sale' price.

"Do you have a job for me?" Robert asked pensively over the phone. "I'm making around $16,000 a month but am willing to work for less. Around $15,000 would work for me. I didn't get a retrenchment package so I need the money to support my loans and lifestyle."

I replied that there has been a global headcount freeze for most companies, especially in his industry (which was downsizing to reduce cost) and no one was hiring. Younger IT managers could be hired at a third of his package. Everyone was unsure about how long the recession would last.

"Is there anything? Any other job I could do?" Robert asked. "I can't believe my company fired me. I have been loyal to them, turning down other offers and never returning headhunters' calls. At least my HR department has kindly provided me an 'outplacement' service where I can get some advice on how to find a new job. What can I do?"

I gave Robert some friendly career advice over coffee and we are still good friends today. He is lucky to have survived the ordeal. But he learnt three important lessons that day.

Lesson #1: In today's economy, no job is guaranteed and no job is truly secure

One client, a Chief Executive Officer of a global technology company, once threw his hands up in exasperation, "Why is staff turnover so high in Asia? Does employee loyalty still exist?"

I replied, "Remember when the dotcom bubble burst in 2000, what did your company do?"

"We laid people off," he replied.

"And during the recession following the September 11 Attacks in 2001?" I asked.

"We laid people off," he answered sheepishly.

"And what did your company do during the Severe Acute Respiratory Syndrome (SARS) outbreak in 2003?"

"Okay, okay—I get the picture. It almost seems unreasonable to expect employee loyalty when employers *themselves* are sometimes more loyal to their shareholders than to their staff."

Some say that employee loyalty may even have a detrimental effect on your career. A recent article on *Forbes* headlined: Employees who stay in companies longer than two years get paid 50 percent less. Unless you belong to the top 5 percent of high performing employees in your company, do not expect your company to plan your career for you—you have to take charge and manage it yourself.

Lesson #2: Are your skills and expertise still needed in this job market?

Like your iPhone software, your skills can easily become obsolete and irrelevant without regular updates. Robert did not realise that whatever he could do, a younger technician could probably do it cheaper, faster, and perhaps even a little better. Is your expertise up-to-date? Have you priced yourself out of the market? Can your job be replaced, automated or outsourced?

Lesson #3: You must prepare a Career Strategy™ before, and not after, the axe falls

Learning career skills and developing your Career Strategy *after* you have been retrenched will be doing too little, too late. While outplacement counseling helps you to deal with grief and come to terms with the retrenchment, with a little career planning in advance, the situation could have been avoided altogether. That is why it is important to have a working Career Strategy before that happens to avoid future pink-slip parties.

In today's fast-paced and ultra-competitive economy, the notion of any job being an 'iron rice bowl' is over. And because you have to rely on yourself (and not your employers) to navigate the next decade of your career, you need to take the initiative to chart your own course and move your career in the right direction and at the correct speed. This book will help you to achieve that in a step-by-step manner.

As a headhunter, I listen to my clients' business concerns and help to solve it by identifying the right leaders with the experience and ability to resolve these issues. I approach these qualified candidates and convince them to join my client's company.

During my decade-long career headhunting for senior business leaders, I often come across executives in their mid-thirties to forties who ask the toughest question of their career: *What next?*

Many are successful managers who have been at the top of their careers for the past ten to fifteen years but are pondering their next move: Do I carry on with the same thing for the next two decades or should I move to something completely different? What are my options? How should I proceed?

If these questions sound familiar, this book is for you. It is written with the mid-career executive in mind—someone with fifteen to twenty years of work experience who may be at a career crossroad.

As a seasoned executive search professional, I often wear two hats—primarily as advisor to clients who need the best candidate to achieve the organisation's goals and as a career coach, counselling candidates on whether the job opportunity is right for them.

In that journey, I have become good friends with many candidates and have also learnt a great deal about career planning from successful clients. This book will cover both perspectives, providing a framework for career planning and strategies to move forward in your career. The tools introduced will help you to discover yourself and some of these personal questions will require deeper thought. I will also provide examples of real-life career stories of senior executives (although their names have been altered for confidentiality).

Who this book will help

- *If you are an undergraduate,* the book is an ideal 'primer' into career-planning, helping to keep you aware of issues that will affect the next forty years of your working life.
- *If you are in your early thirties,* this book will point out the factors that affect your marketability and help you start

planning for your career. It also helps to identify the speed bumps and potholes ahead so you will be able to navigate and avoid them.

- *If you are a mid-career executive in your early forties,* this book will help you develop a personalised Career Strategy to stay relevant and sustainable for the next half of your career.
- *If you are in your fifties,* this book provides a framework for you to attach your own career experiences, useful for mentoring your staff about their own career moves.

It is my hope that by sharing my thoughts and experiences with you, you will be better equipped to embark on that journey of self-discovery and achieve career-fulfillment.

Why read *Career Crossroads*

I am a headhunter with CTPartners, one of the top US-listed executive search firms in the world. In my decade-long career adventure in headhunting, I have successfully placed CEOs and senior business leaders of Fortune 500 companies including Shell, Samsung, Coca-Cola and many others.

I have been fascinated by people's career choices from a young age. I wanted to be a fireman, a doctor and even a teacher. As I got older, I realised that many of my peers had no idea what they wanted to be and chose their careers based on what their parents wanted them to be ("You must be a lawyer, son!") or let their friends make that decision for them ("Hey, let's all sign up for nursing, Bob!"). Worse still are those who follow convention and let the system decide for them ("As the top student, Sally, you have to opt for medicine!").

I loved and excelled in biology so I wanted to embark on a medical career. Unfortunately, I threw up whenever I saw blood. One day, I watched Michael Douglas in the 1987 movie

Wall Street doing his Gordon Gecko "Greed is good" speech and I was hooked! I decided to go to business school instead.

I never looked back. I graduated from the National University of Singapore's business school with an Honours degree and started my career in Shell Eastern Petroleum under their Management Development Programme. I was fast-tracked and exposed to numerous functions of the business. In 2000, I left to start my own digital marketing business.

In 2004, I faced my first career crossroad as I realised that at thirty-two, I had a long road ahead of me but no clear direction. Do I stay in my new industry or return to my old one? Do I move into another start-up or re-join a large multi-national company?

This bothered me because I had a great start to my career, but how would I sustain that momentum? Was I in the right industry? Was I acquiring the right skills to see me through the next two decades of working life? I was perplexed because there were no books on this topic that I could turn to for advice. Even my well-meaning friends gave me great-sounding but clichéd advice like 'follow your heart' and 'only time will tell'.

Worse of all, I did not really have a career mentor to seek advice from. After thinking long and hard, I decided to approach the problem like I would a business issue—by developing a strategy and action plan. I created a very rudimentary framework for career planning and applied it to my situation. The way forward was to leverage my passion for career-counselling, my strength in the sale of professional services and love of meeting new people, and begin a career in executive search.

So I made a strategic career move into Retained Executive Search in 2004 and have not looked back. Today, I am enjoying a fulfilled career as a respected headhunter, career coach, husband to an amazing wife and loving father of two beautiful children. I am also volunteering my services as a council-member of the Singapore Cancer Society, returning my blessings to the community that has given me so many opportunities.

Over the years, I have further refined this career planning model by incorporating my observations of career paths from successful executives and sagely advice from the Chief Executive Officers and vice-presidents I have worked with. I feel that I am now ready to share these strategies with you.

Are you at a career crossroad today? I hope this book will be able to help you navigate through your journey and emerge more successful.

How this book is structured

In the first and second chapters, I introduce the definition of a 'career' and how the concept has changed over the years. I frame your career as a 'journey' in life and show the major milestones that you will make, including the two career crossroads that many encounter. I will elaborate these two decision points in greater detail and offer some basic strategies to manage it.

Chapter 3 explores the concept of a Career Strategy—what it is, why it is imperative that you have one and how to go about developing your own unique strategy. This chapter will set you on the path of self-discovery by taking a hard-nosed look at whether you are headed in the direction that you want.

Chapter 4 visits the reasons for staying in your current job or leaving for better opportunities. Each move has its own costs and benefits. This book provides a checklist and framework for deciding which reasons are truly valid and which are not. This section will help you to decide whether it is time to start looking for something better.

If you have made up your mind to move, Chapter 5 considers the various ways you can do so. A straightforward move like joining a competitor is a low risk endeavour. But what if you are bored or tired of your industry or role? How would you reinvent your career with as little risk as possible? The Career PLAN framework introduced in Chapter 6 will help you to leverage on your strengths to pivot into a different industry or role in a more strategic manner.

After figuring out the specific direction you would like to take, you cannot sit back and wait for the right opportunity to come— it might take too long or may never happen at all. Chapter 7 shows you how to be proactive in your quest for that dream job. It includes both the time-tested strategies for self-marketing and job-targeting, as well as other out-of-the-box ideas.

With a Career Strategy, a Career PLAN and job search strategies in place, you need to develop your own attention-grabbing marketing collaterals—how do you tell your Career Story in the best practice Curriculum Vitae (CV) format. Chapter 8 is peppered with insider-tips on resume writing that only a seasoned headhunter could know.

Once your CV is noticed for the right reasons, Chapter 9 on interview strategies will demonstrate how to deliver the best performance of your life, preparing you for the only three questions that really matter.

Chapter 10 addresses the often asked question of how much of a salary increment to expect. This book provides a realistic framework for evaluating the offer so that both you and your new employer will feel good about it.

Having won the hiring manager over with your success stories, you have finally been made the offer. But how do you decide if this job is really the right one for you? Chapter 11 presents a detailed checklist for you to consider before putting your signature on the dotted line.

After contemplating and accepting the offer, Chapter 12 will walk you through the daunting task of tendering your resignation—the right steps to take and the wrong ones to avoid. It will show you how to handle counter-offers your HR department may give, and a list of things to do or not to do, so as to avoid any legal trouble thereafter.

Chapter 13 will give tips on what to do when a headhunter calls—how you should react, what do you ask and what not to do—while Chapter 14 covers what to do if you are retrenched and offer strategies to get back into the workforce. The conclusion will then summarise the important lessons to take with you.

This book will force you to think about the hard truths and help you to make painful decisions that would pay off in the long run. There are also extra reading materials and links to our online resource at www.career-strategy.com where fresh articles are updated regularly.

Now, on to our first chapter!

BONUS MATERIAL

You will see a Bonus Material icon in the chapters. For more detailed information and examples, visit www.career-strategy. com/bonus and key in the article code to access the extra information.

Chapter 1

Your career

Many of us are defined largely by our careers. Imagine a social gathering where you are meeting people for the first time. After the customary exchange of names, the question 'What do you do for a living?' is likely to come up next. We spend a large part of our lives at work or thinking about work, so our careers are an important aspect of our lives. You do not need to be a high-flying banker or a top-notch lawyer to be defined by what you do. Even a homemaker will proudly state her job as a 'stay-at-home-mom' and *not* a 'housewife'.

A great number of people lost their jobs during the financial crisis in 2008. Speaking to many of them, it was evident that losing a job hits the men particularly badly, even when they were not the sole breadwinners. Some kept their spouses in the dark, pretending to go to work even though it was the daily visit to their outplacement counsellor. They felt that losing their job felt like a loss of their place in the house and affected their self-worth. It didn't matter that they received a generous retrenchment package or had enough savings to tide them through the crisis; it wasn't the money. It was an emotion, and that is how much a career could mean.

Another way of looking at your career

If you are a mid-career executive and have worked for more than fifteen years, what is your biggest asset?

It could be that beautiful house you are staying in—but is it owned by you or your bank? Or that shiny sports car in your garage—is a car even an asset? It could even be that exotic stock portfolio managed by your Swiss private banker—but as recent recessions and market corrections have repeatedly demonstrated, the value of these assets fluctuate and could even be wiped out overnight. Property markets have collapsed and banks have also gone under. Even if the markets do not crash and your money in the bank is safe—in today's world of low interest rates, the returns on these assets could be quite paltry. So, think again—are these things really your greatest asset?

There is one asset you own that continues to pay regular monthly dividends, and if managed correctly, will be able to grow and increase in value and payouts in the future. This asset is your career and the monthly dividends are your salary.

I realised this during the financial crisis as my personal stock portfolio was decimated by the merciless market. Years of painstaking savings were wiped out in weeks and it felt terrible. However, a constant stream of funds still came in despite the massacre—it was my salary, derived from the job I still had.

Once we start to view our careers as assets, we begin to understand how important it is to us. It also sets us thinking about acquiring an asset-enhancing strategy to help improve its longevity, relevance, value and yield. If this asset is neglected, it could lose its value and may never get fully back on track.

A property investor would not hesitate to spend money on asset-enhancing activities like adding a fresh coat of paint. He will also think twice before renting a place out to rowdy students who could cause more damage than the deposit can cover. Similarly, a wise executive who views his career as an asset will know that he needs a strategy to ensure it remains valuable and increases in value over time. This could take the form of making smart career moves to bigger companies or on to better roles.

He will also avoid short-sighted activities that could jeopardise his value or market demand, such as refusing to upgrade his skills or electing to remain in a sunset industry.

So remember two important concepts as we move forward:
- Your career is your biggest long-term asset.
- Your monthly salary is the monthly dividend from this asset.

What is a career?

In the past, a career was considered to be "the work you did for a company." This was during the time when people hardly left their companies and spent most of their lives doing the same job with a single employer. However, in today's knowledge-based economy, a career is defined as "the evolving sequence of a person's work experience over time" by Arthur, Hall & Lawrence in *The handbook of career theory* in 1989. This has two key implications:

1. You have *one* career that could comprise of several jobs during your life, and
2. This career is constantly evolving.

In the past, an employee who has worked for twenty years in the same company would have been described as 'stable' or 'loyal'. Today, that same person could be rudely described as 'deadwood' or 'part of the furniture'. How times have changed!

A career journey

Our career journey is the pathway we take from childhood to retirement and consists of various stages.

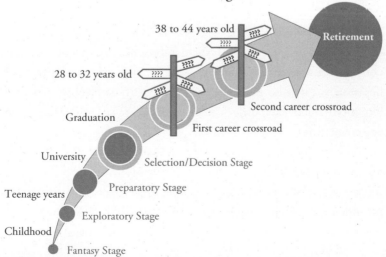

Stage 1: Fantasy Stage

As young children, we probably recall wanting to be a fireman, astronaut or an actor. These fantasies are an important first step in our thought processes regarding our desired roles in society and our perceptions of what constitutes a good job and what we find interesting. It is a useful phase because it clues us in on the sort of role that would make us truly happy in life. There can be no limits to a child's imagination when it comes to career selection. A successful CEO once shared that his childhood fantasy was to be a garbage collector because he thought it was great fun riding at the back of a garbage truck.

Stage 2: Exploratory Stage

This stage starts from between twelve to eighteen, when we explore more realistic career ideas. This phase allows us the latitude to evaluate options and narrow down the wide spectrum of options to a realistic few that would be of interest to us. More importantly, it not only tells us what we would like to be, but what roles or industries we *don't* want to be in.

Stage 3: Preparation Stage

By eighteen, we would have a general idea of which direction our interests lie and will enroll ourselves into the faculty of our choice at a selected university. This is, however, not the final decision we will be making. Even in highly specialised courses like medicine or law, other career options are still relatively open at graduation.

This stage prepares us with the specialised training and knowledge required to qualify or equip us for the role we will undertake upon graduation. The college education process also provides the insight into whether the course is in line with our choices and is suitable for our personalities, temperaments and abilities. For example, after five years of medical school, one friend decided to be a clinical researcher, much to the dismay of his parents who had sponsored his half-a-million-dollar education abroad.

Stage 4: Selection/Decision

Upon graduation, we need to decide which direction our lives will take. If you are the lucky few with top scores and really know what you want to be, this crossroad will be as easy as deciding which offer to accept. However, for many others, the choice of their first job depends largely a *circumstance-based selection*—the truth is that we often end up in our very first job as a result of whichever company decided to open one of our numerous 'application for employment' emails, interview us, and make us an offer. I joined Shell Eastern Petroleum as a management trainee because fifteen other companies had rejected my applications.

This circumstance-based selection is hardly strategic or intelligent in nature but is a reflection of how most of us landed our first jobs. As a result, many of us may have ended up in an industry that we might not have the passion for or in a role that is less satisfying. For some, it is a great opportunity to learn about a new industry and provides insights into whether this would make a good lifelong career. Nevertheless, we still trudge on for about five to eight years till we hit our first career crossroad.

REAL-LIFE CAREER STORY

Jeremy, 43, Medical Director, US-based drug company

Jeremy was a candidate I met. He shared that he never quite knew what he wanted to be as a kid, but he knew that he didn't want to be a medical doctor. Both his parents were doctors. His father was a trauma surgeon and his mother a gynaecologist. He never liked the fact that they were seldom around and detested the abrupt way they would leap up and run out of the house the moment their pagers went off, even on weekends.

You can imagine the pressure he faced when applying for a place at university. His parents pressured him to go to medical school even though he really didn't want to. But what could a helpless nineteen-year-old do? He reluctantly acquiesced and spent the next five years there, followed by another two years of internship. When he completed his obligations, he was much older and had learnt how to be his own man.

He sat his parents down and said, "Mom, Dad, I did what you want. I'm a doctor now—but I don't wish to practise medicine as I have no interest in seeing sick people every day for the rest of my life. I'm going to find a medical-related job in the corporate world."

Jeremy shared, "I remember that day very clearly because I felt so liberated. I signed up with a pharmaceutical company as a sales representative, drawing a salary that was half of what I would have received at the hospital—but I loved it!"

Fast forward fifteen years and today, he is a regional director heading a team of twenty. "I feel that I have made the right move and found my true passion."

What advice would he give?

"I think firstly, know what you want in life—and even if you don't, keep trying to find out by striving to know yourself. Secondly, it's never too late to change course. Your career is never linear—it is a journey that snakes along and sometimes, even brings you back to the start. And thirdly, keep pressing on and never give up."

BONUS MATERIAL

How do you know if a career/vocation/profession is the right one? Visit www.career-strategy.com/bonus and key "Vocation" to access this extra article.

Chapter 2

The career crossroads

Joseph was the Asia-Pacific Managing Director of a large US-based software company with over a thousand staff. At 41, he had enjoyed a meteoric rise to his current position after a rapid series of promotions and was seen by many as a rock-star. He had trebled the business in as many years and was widely admired by his peers in the industry.

Even at the top of his game, he felt that something was not quite right. He enjoyed what he was doing but could not see himself doing this for the next two decades, and it was eating him up. He was frustrated because as a business leader, he spent countless meetings rallying the troops about how wonderful the company was and how exciting the industry would be, while deep down inside, he was thinking of leaving the industry or the company; and that made him feel like a hypocrite.

Joseph felt trapped and wanted to do something about it, but the demands of his job meant that he had to keep his eye on the ball and spent more time figuring out how to achieve next quarter's targets instead of thinking of a solution to his career crisis. He sighed, "If only I had a magic eight-ball to tell me what to do next. What are my options and how do I manage the second-half of my career?"

Joseph was a candidate that I had placed many years back. His story is common and resonates with many mid-career executives in their early forties. After years of meeting senior executives in my headhunting career, I noticed a common pattern emerging. Many of them go through one or two periods of intense self-questioning regarding their career direction and long-term planning. These executives are top performers but yet they still ask themselves, "What's next?"

The first mini crisis usually occurs when they are around 28 to 32 years old, roughly five to eight years into their working life—the *first career crossroad*. Some people do not experience this first crossroad at all, jumping directly into their *second career crossroad* at the 38- to 44-year-old mark.

The first career crossroad

The first career crossroad is marked by the questions: Do I like this company? Is this the industry I want to be in? Am I enjoying this business/job?

Having spent five to eight years in a job/industry that you had gotten into by some stroke of luck, you are not wrong to wonder whether there are better things outside—a missed opportunity, a more dynamic and exciting industry you would rather be in or even consider starting a business. These are valid questions and many 30-year-olds face this situation, wondering whether to move forward, sideways, or even backwards.

One candidate I met was a Mensa-certified genius who graduated top of his Ivy League college and had spent the first six years of his life in top US consultancy firms. He had performed spectacularly in his role and was in line for a partnership. But at thirty, he was mentally burnt out. The 85 percent travel schedule, late-night teleconferences and countless reports generated took a toll on his mental health and he started to wonder whether there were better career options. He even considered setting up a childcare centre for a change. Yet another 32-year-old candidate, who was a trained lawyer, started thinking, "I'm totally bored reading hundred-page contracts—maybe I don't want to be a lawyer after all. Are there other non-legal roles out there?"

Here are some strategies to handle your first career crossroad:

- *Think long term.* Is your industry promising? Is it growing or is it in decline? If you are in a fast-growing sectors like cloud computing or social-networking, then there will be a lot of potential for new opportunities. However, if you are in a sunset-industry like manufacturing where all such activities are moving to China or Myanmar, then you really need to think hard about staying in the business. As you are still relatively early in your career, you can exit your industry and move to one with more potential.

- *How about making your job more exciting?* If you are feeling bored by your current job, how about increasing your job scope? You could try volunteering for new projects or even taking on a regional portfolio just to enhance your expertise and marketability.

- *Have you considered upgrading?* The time may be just right to get that masters you had always wanted. Being in the early thirties has its advantages in that your opportunity cost for a year off work is not too high and you do get better mileage building your MBA networks earlier in your career.

- *Ever considered taking a short break?* Take some time off to do something you always wanted to do—scale a mountain or backpack through Europe (now that you actually have some money). The fresh air and time alone will give you the much-needed clarity to think your next steps through. It could also recharge your batteries to drive into the next phase of your career, re-energising your spirit for the challenges ahead.

- *How about trying something different?* Maybe the time might be right for you to try out the idea at the back of your mind. It could be an innovative business idea or a social enterprise. It could also be a bold career move into a completely unrelated field you've always been passionate about but never dared to explore. The advantage of being young is that you could always revert to your old line of work if things do not work out. As they say, nothing ventured, nothing gained. Who knows?

As you are in the early stages of your career, this first career crossroad gives you a good opportunity to re-evaluate your options and plan a forward strategy before you become too entrenched in your industry or role. If approached correctly, it could be a useful first-step in calibrating your Career Strategy.

The second career crossroad

The second career crossroad is trickier to navigate because being in the 38 to 45 age group could be the make-or-break moment in your life. At this stage, you probably have a family with young children and perhaps a home loan or two, so the risks of taking a wrong turn will come at a higher cost. Being in this demographic group, your career runway is much shorter and you may have fewer opportunities to correct a mistake.

Much like Joseph (introduced at the beginning), the executive facing his second career crossroad starts thinking: "I've had a successful career all my life. I've performed exceedingly well in my job for the past fifteen years and am a successful senior executive or top contributor in my organisation. I'm well-liked and respected by colleagues and others in the industry. I'm at the top of my career and have learnt everything I've needed about this business and achieved everything I've set out to do. Everything is going well. Although I love my work and industry, I don't want to spend the next twenty years of my life doing this. I wonder what the next phase in my life holds for me."

This question becomes even more poignant for many because turning 45 marks a symbolic midway mark of one's career. Most of us started work right after we completed our undergraduate degree which puts us around 21 to 25 years of age. Given a retirement age of 65, it means that our career spans approximately forty years—we spend up to four decades of our life working. And if you were to calculate a mid-way point of in year twenty, that would put our mid-career mark at around age 45.

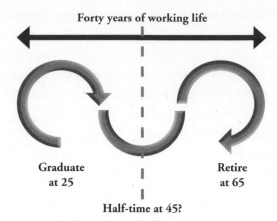

Now, have you ever seen a soccer match without a half-time? That is why many consider this to be the half-time mark where we head back to the locker room, charge up and reconsider our game-plan for the second half (the next two decades) of the game.

This is a seminal moment in your life and could affect your entire future, so do not take it lightly. In my experience, people do make mistakes at this critical juncture—here are three of the most common ones.

Mistake #1: Listening to advice from friends
The people around us love us and are well-meaning, but often, they are simply not qualified to give career advice. If you wake up one morning and discover a mysterious golf ball-sized lump at the back of your neck, would you ask your colleague what his opinion is? Would you let him operate on you? Likewise, not everyone is qualified to give the right career advice. You might end up with bad clichés like 'follow your passion' or 'do what you love'. Not all passions will pay the bill and in any great job, there will always be elements that you dislike.

Mistake #2: Listening to your heart, not your head

Many people facing their second career crisis could already be feeling quite frustrated by their situation and may be unable to keep a clear mind when making decisions. As a result, the actions are a result of emotional rather than rational decisions. One bank manager was so frustrated with his work that he resigned and started a hipster café a month later, even though he did not have any experience in that business. You should always think with clarity before deciding what to do. So take a few deep breaths and calm down before making a decision.

Mistake #3: Not taking enough time or making an effort to learn how to manage this career crisis

The worst thing to do at this stage is to do nothing at all. Some people freeze like a deer caught in the headlights and hope the problem goes away, whilst other bury their head in the sand like the proverbial ostrich. Denial is your worst enemy. Some executives are so busy with their own work and job demands that they do not even have the time to realise that they are actually in the midst of a crisis, let alone figure out how to handle one. You need to extricate yourself from your current situation—even if only for an afternoon—to sit by the beach or pool to take stock of your current situation.

It is great that you are reading this book now as it shows that you have taken the first step and have started educating yourself on how to navigate these perilous waters. So if you feel that you are at a career crossroad right now, do not fret for you are not alone.

If you are *not* at a career-crossroad, then this would be the ideal time for you to learn as well, for you may be encountering one very soon and will be equipped to handle it when that time comes.

REAL-LIFE CAREER STORY

Philippe, 38, Entrepreneur

One candidate, Philippe, was born in Finland and moved to the United States when he was eight years old, staying in the beautiful Florida Keys. Immediately after he graduated from an Ivy League business school, he worked for a technology start-up in the Silicon Valley—those were the heady days when Jerry Yang (Yahoo!) and Sabeer Bhatia (Hotmail) were the movers and shakers in the industry.

The company he worked for never made it to the big leagues and failed, but the lessons he learned taught him how to run a technology business. He then worked with IBM for a couple of years before realising that it was not the life he wanted.

So he quit in 2005 and started his own dotcom. It was both scary and fun and after six years of blood and sweat, he managed to sell it off in 2011 for a tidy eight-digit figure. As he was the largest shareholder, most of it went to him and he exited the business altogether.

What did he do with his money? Being an avid sailor, he treated himself by buying a luxury yacht, loaded his wife and two daughters (two- and four-years old at the time) and sailed around the world for the next three years.

He shared that he had enough money to retire comfortably but wanted some stability for the girls, so last year, he sold the yacht and settled down in Melbourne, Australia.

He felt that he had achieved much in the first half of my career, but paid a high price as well—his health suffered and his wife almost left him because she said that he was married to his job. After mending fences with her in the past three years whilst sailing the world, he feels he is now ready to embark on the next half of his career.

He has some wild ideas in mind—probably another start-up or two, but he doesn't really need the money so is not as willing to go through the pain all over again. He is considering mentoring some start-ups but worries that it might be too small a job.

"It is strange that despite my earlier career success, I am at a career crossroad at this point in time. I can only hope to get some clarity soon."

Chapter 3

The Career Strategy™

Do you eat a lot of carbohydrates in your meal or do you load up on proteins instead? Do you save for a rainy day or do you invest more money in stocks or property? If you have an exercise plan, do you perform cardio-workouts more than resistance-training, or is it the other way around? When you park your car in a crowded mall, do you park your car at the first available lot even though it is the furthest from the elevator lobby, or will you hover around the lobby, waiting for a driver to retrieve his vehicle so you can grab his spot?

Many of us have mental models for each decision-making process in our life. We have diet strategies to ensure we eat healthily, investment strategies so that we get the maximum yield for our hard-earned money, and exercise strategies so that we can have optimal results for our hard work at the gym. We even have parking strategies when going to the mall—for men, it is the lot nearest to the elevators; for ladies, pretty much anywhere. So, I am often perplexed to discover that so many executives do not even have a Career Strategy.

As a headhunter, I have studied the careers of various business leaders, both illustrious and otherwise. In my research, I have noted that there is one common thread among those who have been successful in their careers. They all had a Career Strategy which they had developed and adhered closely to. They had a vision and a plan, which helped them to map out their strategies.

Executives who did not make time to develop their own strategies found themselves derailed when negative events or unexpected opportunities suddenly appear. When they are approached by a headhunter for a once-in-a-lifetime opportunity, they will have no clue whether it is right for them; or when their division is shut down because the operations have moved to China. Often, these executives only think of their

Career Strategy when they are facing retrenchment or after—which is doing too little too late. Your Career Strategy should be a live document that is constantly updated and upgraded as you progress along your career journey. With a coherent Career Strategy to guide your path, navigating obstacles and seizing long-term advantages becomes clearer, and the way forward is easier.

What is a Career Strategy™?

> A CAREER STRATEGY IS A PLAN YOU DEVELOP BASED ON SELF-KNOWLEDGE AND MARKET TRENDS, IDENTIFYING YOUR STRENGTHS, WEAKNESSES, PASSION AND VALUES, AS WELL AS VARIOUS MARKET OPPORTUNITIES AND THREATS LOOMING ON YOUR HORIZON.

Your Career Strategy is about self-discovery and should provide a roadmap of where you would like to be *two jobs* down the road and *how* you are going to get there.

Why have a Career Strategy™?

Many executives are only thinking about their 'next move' but lose sight of the bigger picture—the long-term goal. They ask, "What would I like to do for my next job?" rather than 'What skills do I need for my future role (seven years down the road) and will this next job provide me with the skills, depth, expertise and knowledge for that?"

Pictorially, instead of targeting what the next job should be, You should be thinking of what you envision yourself to be in seven to ten years' time (eg. CEO), and start analysing what attributes the next job should have that would give you the skills, networks, expertise and knowledge to prepare you for that role.

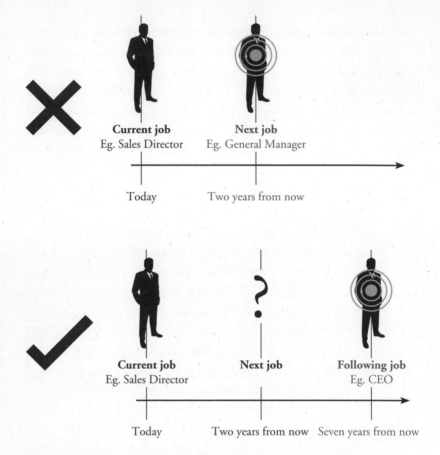

Sometimes, the job opportunity presented by your headhunter may seem ideal from a short-term perspective; but if you are looking at your Career Strategy from a two-jobs-down perspective, it might not make sense at all. Sometimes, it could even hurt your professional branding—these include accepting a laid-back job posting when you are too young or working for a company with a bad industry reputation.

How to develop a Career Strategy™

Seek an experienced career coach to sit down and work with you. And by career coach, I do not mean an outplacement counsellor who usually counsels retrenched staff. The best career coaches come in two forms.

The first is a *career mentor* who is a senior or retired business leader who has had an illustrious career in your current industry or in your function. If you are a finance manager, a Chief Finance Officer of a larger company would be ideal, as he would possess the wisdom of experience and understand the dynamics of your industry. Often, this could even be your former boss.

The other type of ideal career coach would a seasoned *executive search professional* or a *headhunter* who specialises in your industry, as he understands your sector and knows what future-skills are required. Headhunters with many years of experience are the best career coaches around as they spend a lot of time counseling their candidates, offering career advice and walking them through the entire job-switching process.

There are also forms of career coaches out there who may take the shape of retired HR managers, recently-retrenched executives, amongst others. If you have to, choose cautiously— select the one you feel is most qualified to handle your situation and provide learned advice.

If you are would like to take a DIY approach, you could use the framework recommended in the next chapter.

REAL-LIFE CAREER STORY

Jack Welch, former CEO, General Electric

Everybody knows Jack Welch, the famous CEO who grew General Electric from a US$26.8 billion company when he took over as CEO in 1980, to a US$130 billion company in 2000 when he left. If you had invested $10,000 in his company when he started, you would have had a $710,500 nest-egg when he left twenty years later!

But did you know that Jack was actually 'Dr Jack Welch'? He had earned a Masters and a PhD in Chemical Engineering from the University of Illinois in 1960, a year before he joined GE.

In his book, *Jack: Straight From The Gut*, he shared that he had deliberately kept that fact a secret from others in the company when he signed up, because he had a very clear Career Strategy.

He realised that if everyone called him 'Dr Welch', he would be positioned (at a very early stage of his career) on a technical/engineering track, rather than on a management track, which was what he wanted. Had he been developed into further technical roles, he knew that his career options would be very limited. However, once he was placed on the Management Development program, he knew his outcomes would be far more promising.

So he insisted on having everyone "Just call me Jack!"—and the rest as they say, is history!

As you can see, Jack Welch had the foresight to look far ahead, in fact, several jobs down the road and make the right decisions very early in his career that led him to be recognised later in life as the 'Manager of the Century' by *Fortune* Magazine in 1999.

Chapter 4

Developing your
Career Strategy™

One of the most important lessons I learnt as a young management trainee in Shell was a group exercise called 'Lost at Sea'. A popular team-building game, it involves imagining a scenario where you are on a cruise with some friends and your yacht springs a leak in the middle of the ocean. You can only bring *four* items onto your rescue raft. The list of items include:

- Army rations (food)
- Bottle of rum
- Can of shark repellent
- Carton of chocolate bars
- Fishing kit
- Five-gallon container of drinking water
- Flare gun
- GPS tracker
- Half-gallon gasoline and lighter
- Mobile phone
- Mosquito net
- Nylon rope
- Oars
- Shaving mirror
- Small transistor radio
- Twenty-square-foot white canvas sheet

Which items would you choose? Each piece of equipment has its own use and will be difficult to prioritise over each other. The transistor radio could keep your survivors' morale up but we could say the same for the bottle of rum which would also double up as a disinfectant. Likewise, the chocolate bars would be a great source of energy but was it better than a fishing kit you could use over and over again?

At the end of the exercise, we were told to present our team's solution and explain our reasons. The teams had quite mixed results but somehow, almost every team selected the rum—I wonder why.

The trainer then paused and told us something that blew our minds. He said, "I confess this is a trick assignment. This was not an exercise in what item to choose but in what strategy to adopt. Right off the bat, I saw that everyone started picking items based on what they thought were most important. However, you should not have started with the picking of items. You should have begun by discussing the master strategy you want to adopt, then selecting the items that support that strategy.

A master strategy could be 'survive', 'facilitate rescue' or even 'row your way home'. If you managed to 'may-day' your last known location and know that help is on the way, or are confident of rescue within days, then choose the 'facilitate rescue' strategy. Select equipment that could expedite your tiny life-raft being located. You could choose the mirror (for daytime-signaling to rescue aircraft), gasoline and lighter (for night-signaling), the flare gun and probably water (rather than food). However, if you are unsure if people even know you are missing, your master strategy would be to 'survive as long as you can'. You would then stockpile the army rations, water, fishing kit and canvas for protection against the elements so that you can last as long as possible to await rescue, if it even comes."

He reiterated, "First, have a master strategy, then decide on your tactics. If you allow the tail to wag the dog, you are doomed."

We learnt that day onwards that in Shell, every decision you made had to be dictated by a master strategy—what we call the big-picture or helicopter-view. Likewise, when you craft your own Career Strategy, you must have the big picture of all the variables in your mind so you can see which is the best master strategy to adopt—and the big picture looks like this:

An overview of your Career Strategy™

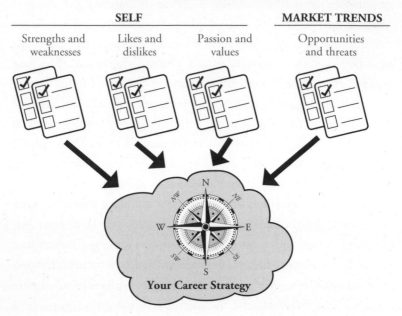

SELF			MARKET TRENDS
Strengths and weaknesses	Likes and dislikes	Passion and values	Opportunities and threats

Your Career Strategy

The first step is self-discovery

To begin, you need to take an honest look at yourself and understand where your strengths, weaknesses and passion lies. You also need to know what you really like and dislike in a job. Having a good understanding of your temperament will also help because some jobs require very specific temperaments to be successful.

Discovering yourself

Strengths and weaknesses

Likes and dislikes

Passion and values

Strengths and weaknesses

Knowing what you are really good (or terrible) at gives you an edge in crafting out your ideal career. For instance, if you are very good at making new friends and influencing people, you would probably find a sales role somewhat satisfying. Or if you are really good with numbers, perhaps an analytical or finance role will fit you better. However, if you do not have a creative bone in your body and dislike dreaming up new ideas, then a career in marketing may not be the best choice for you.

Weaknesses are not always a liability. These could sometimes be an 'area for further improvement'. Remedying a weakness by learning a new skill or coaching will help you to grow. For instance, George, a 43-year-old sales manager, was not strong in accounting but he had his sights set on a general manager position, so it was a necessary skill to master.

There are many ways to discover this aspect of yourself. You can spend an afternoon at the beach reflecting on your own attributes, ask your peers though a 360-degree feedback exercise or do a psychographic test like the Harrison Assessment to specifically find out what you enjoy doing and are really good at. Visit www.career-strategy.com for more information.

Discovering your strengths and weaknesses

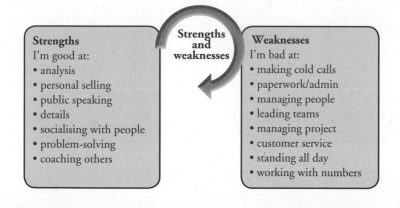

Strengths
I'm good at:
• analysis
• personal selling
• public speaking
• details
• socialising with people
• problem-solving
• coaching others

Strengths and weaknesses

Weaknesses
I'm bad at:
• making cold calls
• paperwork/admin
• managing people
• leading teams
• managing project
• customer service
• standing all day
• working with numbers

Likes and dislikes

Let's face it—there are some things we really wish we could wave away with a magic wand. For some, this includes administrative paperwork, repetitive physical work or collecting overdue debts from bad paymasters. For others, it may include cold-calling, personal selling, crunching numbers or even public speaking.

We will not do well in roles that require us to do things we do not like because we naturally avoid or procrastinate doing such tasks. Having a better understanding of what you like and dislike provides an interesting insight into your ideal job. Often, these are a result of our experiences with our current or previous job experiences.

An easy way of uncovering what you dislike doing is to ask yourself the following question: In my current role, I wish I had *less* … (perhaps bureaucracy, paperwork, travel or people-management?) Conversely, to find out what you like doing, ask yourself: In my next role, I wish I had *more* … (perhaps a diverse product portfolio, global exposure or operational experience?) Then use these answers to draw up your own list.

Discovering your likes and dislikes

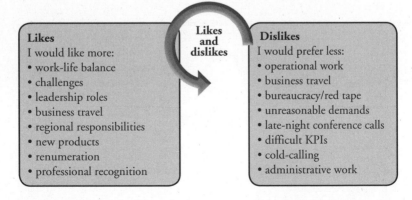

Likes
I would like more:
- work-life balance
- challenges
- leadership roles
- business travel
- regional responsibilities
- new products
- renumeration
- professional recognition

Likes and dislikes

Dislikes
I would prefer less:
- operational work
- business travel
- bureaucracy/red tape
- unreasonable demands
- late-night conference calls
- difficult KPIs
- cold-calling
- administrative work

Passion and values

It is easy to overlook this aspect when we evaluate our life-goals or career plans. What do you stand for? What do you stand against? What goes against the grain of your personal (or religious) belief system? It is important to articulate your value system clearly, instead of leaving it as a poorly defined list of 'maybes'. Values can be viewed as personal and corporate.

Personal values

Most successful executives feel that their jobs should be congruent with their personal values, otherwise, they may never be at peace with themselves and this feeling may slowly rob them of any joy they have in the role. One of the key questions is whether the industry you are in or are about to join shares your values. There are individuals who refuse to work for tobacco or gambling companies simply on the principle that these industries are unwholesome and thrive off the misery of fellow human beings. No matter what the salary or perks may be, drawing a salary whose source is inevitably derived from the suffering of others might seem offensive to some.

Besides the type of industry, the type of role would also matter. Some individuals find it troubling to sell time-share or multi-level-marketing products as they do not fully subscribe to that business model. Sometimes, your values may be deeply personal but could also extend to the people whom you work with. Does your boss or team you work with share your values? Do they respect each other in an encouraging a manner like you do, or is it a very impersonal, performance-driven environment that is harsh to mistakes and non-performers?

Work-life balance can also be an important value to consider. From flexi-time to unrecorded family leave and work-from-home arrangements—how much of it would you like and will the company agree? If you are planning to start a family within the next three years, you may want more family time. But if your children have grown up and you can devote more time and energy to the business, you wouldn't mind a less family-friendly working environment. Sometimes, the degree of work-life balance could even be a deal-breaker for your new role depending on the phase of life you are in.

Corporate values

Your personal values should also extend to the company you work for. Does the organisation reflect the values you subscribe to? Is it active in supporting the environment or champion the rights of women? There is some pride in working for a socially responsible brand like the Body Shop or Ben & Jerry's.

On a micro-level, the culture of the company needs to be congruent with your personal values. Is this company known for its meat-grinding, hire and fire culture of unbridled corporate greed like some large financial institutions? One finance director refused to work for another family-run billion-dollar regional conglomerate because they had, allegedly, three sets of accounts and made him sign off dubious statements and reports. He said, "I wanted to be able to sleep at night and what they wanted me to do went against my principles. I also didn't want to go to jail."

Some executives with a long career history in multinational companies (MNCs) may have reservations about fitting into the culture of an small and medium enterprise (SME), worrying that it would be run too 'locally' and that their value systems may not be as progressive as their larger counterparts. On the flip side, they could have had enough of the large, monolithic and bureaucratic system and prefer to work in a smaller, more personal setting that an SME can offer. Your list of personal and corporate values could look like this:

Discovering your values

Personal	Values	Corporate
• Not working for a tobacco or gambling-related company • Professional and personal integrity • A healthy work-life balance		• A respectful environment • A company that values employees • A socially responsible company

What are you passionate about?

"The only way to do great work is to love what you do."

—STEVE JOBS

If you were asked to name the teachers who have left the deepest impression on you, chances are that less than five names would come to mind. These teachers inspired and never gave up on you. They made their lessons came alive with their way of energising students, nurturing love for even the most mundane topics. What drove those wonderful teachers to such inspiring levels?

It is passion. If you are fortunate enough to be in a job or industry you are passionate about, you are probably enjoying every moment of it. If you aren't already energised by your current job, switching to an industry you are passionate about could re-energise your focus and bring more meaning to life.

One retired army officer was very passionate about golf and would spend most afternoons on the greens perfecting his sport. After some months, he decided to start a company to organise golfing trips overseas and trade in golfing equipment. He decided that his next role would be passion-led and never looked back. He said, "When you are doing what you are passionate about, it isn't work!"

One of the main reasons why I ventured into executive search was because I have always been passionate about career coaching. To this day, I wake up every Monday energised by the week's work ahead, knowing how many lives I would impact positively in the days ahead.

However, we must be mindful that passion alone may not be enough to pay the bills. We need to be realistic in our expectations and always have a commercial focus to our aspirations, unless you already have an 'exit strategy' with a generous war-chest in place. Your list of things you are passionate about could look like this:

Discovering your passions

Passion

Passions
Things I love doing:
• Public speaking
• Coaching
• Golf/cycling/sports
• Building things
• Creating new ideas
• Meeting new people
• Selling ideas

Market trends

It has been said that if you put a frog into hot water, it will jump out immediately. But if you put it in a comfortably cool pot of water and slowly turn the heat up, it will not notice the rising temperature and will ultimately get slowly cooked. If you are not careful about your career, you might end up being that proverbial boiled frog—slow changes in the surrounding may numb us to big changes in the market. The top electric typewriter salesmen from Olivetti must have thought that the booming typewriter business of the seventies would last forever.

So you need to be aware of the direction your industry is headed. What will the landscape of your industry look like in the next five or ten years? Will it be dis-intermediated by technology, made redundant by automation or replaced by cheap labour? Will the market for your products or services dry up? Some industries we see today may not even be around in the next five years. One example would be brick-and-mortar travel agencies—with the advent of online ticketing, people may find going to a travel agency a hassle. Can you name a few industries that are in a serious state of decline? Knowing the future of your industry will help chart your next few career moves. If it is on the decline, tough decisions will have to be made.

REAL-LIFE CAREER STORY

Antonio, GM, Plastics injection molding company

The plastics sector was one of the fastest growing industries globally in the seventies and eighties. Some parts of it were even regarded as high-technology precision engineering and there was great demand for talents in this area. Antonio was one of the early movers in the industry. He graduated with a production engineering degree and immediately found a job as a production manager in the burgeoning plastics injection molding industry. He made good money in the first ten years of his career as he rode the upward wave of his industry and was made operations director at 33. His career was on a roll.

However, cheaper alternative locations emerged in China and Mexico in the nineties, with costs a fraction of what it took to make the same products at home. Advance in automation and increase in quality control at these foreign plants made the 'we have superior product quality here' argument untenable. Ultimately, the plants in developed countries shut down as production shifted to China or Mexico. In those days, the prevailing theme for companies was 'emigrate or evaporate'.

Tony received his retrenchment notice when his plant shut down in 1996 and everyone was laid off. His competitors were likewise moving their operations and there simply wasn't a market for him any longer. At 33, he had two stark choices—face retrenchment at home or relocate to China for work.

The first option was unpalatable as he would have no salary for an unknown period of time whilst he sought an alternative career. Then, with companies were shifting their operations in China, there was a strong demand for experienced managers to help set up their new factories and train staff. These companies did not mind paying good salaries and even offered expatriate benefits. After all, foreigners with the right work ethic and experience were in strong demand. So Tony uprooted his family and moved to Beijing in 1997.

However, it is a different story in China today. Foreign managers are no longer in demand as local managers (many under the tutelage of the same foreigners) have gained the depth of knowledge or expertise required to run operations. Local talents are cheaper, younger and better-suited to managing their fellow countrymen, supplanting their aging and more expensive mentors. With cost-constraints, these 'expatriate managers' are no longer in demand.

Once again, Tony received another retrenchment notice. This time, the other option was to move to where the new demand for expertise was—manufacturing sites further inland to second- or third-tier cities in China, where the local populace is not sophisticated enough to run operations. These backwater towns are far from ideal, especially for his wife and young children. And because of the same cost-constraints, there would not be expatriate benefits.

Tony realised that even if he took the job, it would only be a three-year extension of his predicament. The locals in those factories would take over his job once he taught them the ropes. His move after that would be even bleaker—and he may have to return home as an older worker with no marketable skills.

Suddenly, Tony realised in hindsight that at 35, he should have seen the writing on the wall in 1996 that the entire industry was in decline and that he should have taken the more painful step of re-training himself and switching to a different industry then.

While hindsight is perfect, with a deeper look at the market trends affecting your industry, you will be better placed to judge where you want to be, *two jobs* down the road, today.

I still remember my final job interview with Shell with much amusement. As a fresh graduate, I was still wet behind the ears and hoping to join a reputable oil company like Shell. I had already passed the infamous eight-hour Assessment Centre, where young aspirants were put through a grueling battery of scenarios and presentations, and had emerged unscathed. The final hurdle was the interview with the marketing director who everyone knew as a hard-nosed business leader. After an hour of intense grilling, he threw me an unexpected curve-ball. He asked whether I thought oil was a 'sunset industry'.

Without time to think, I responded with, "Yes it is—oil will run out someday." He rebutted sternly, "Then why do you want to join an oil company since there's no future?"

I replied cheekily, "Yes, oil is a sunset industry, but there's still at least half a century of oil left in the ground—by which time I would be happily retired."

The marketing director burst into laughter saying, "My sentiments exactly! I absolutely agree with you!"

They made me an incredible offer on the spot.

Here are some questions you need to ask when analysing the market trends affecting your business:

Is your industry...
- stable or facing a lot of consolidation? (Such as mega-acquisitions or massive retrenchments)
- heading towards obsolescence? (Such as pagers or hard-disk drives)
- moving to a cheaper location? (Such as in China or Vietnam)
- being replaced by newer technologies in five years time? (Such as LCD screens being replaced by LED monitors)

Is your job...
- being dis-intermediated by newer technology? (Such as recruiters replaced by LinkedIn)
- at risk of being replaced by another function? (Such as Chief Information Officer role being replaced by the Chief Operations Officer)
- at risk of being permanently outsourced? (Such as debt collection)

Are your company's product/services...
- seeing continued demand or sales in slow decline?
- still needed by your clients in five to ten years time?
- discontinued in more mature markets like the US or Europe?

In conclusion, to develop a Career Strategy, you need to understand yourself as well as the market trends in your industry. This is a critical step you need to look, once again, at the big picture presented below. Take the afternoon off to conduct your own analysis—you will find it a good investment of your time.

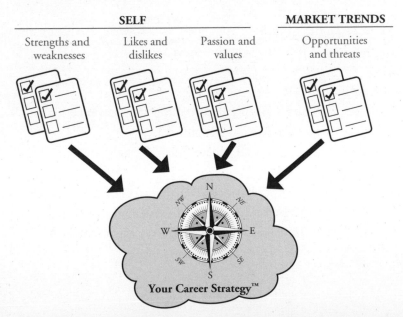

Indeed, for us to have a successful and fulfilling career, we will need to have a coherent Career Strategy, thoughtfully crafted based on one's strengths, passion and market trends. This is a dynamic document that needs to be updated constantly in line with changes to your life-situation and with shifts in the market. The entire concept can be summarised by the popular internet meme.

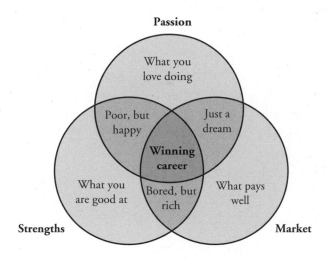

In an ideal world, we would all love to be in the middle intersection, doing what we love, what we are good at and getting paid well for it. However, chances are that we are not. We could be doing what pays really well that we're great at, but it is something we may have lost our passion for along the way.

For the lucky few who are in the middle intersection enjoying their careers, there is still a need to watch out for blind spots in the job market and remember that the environment changes so often that you could be nudged out gradually or even suddenly.

The purpose of a Career Strategy is to move yourself towards the centre of the Venn diagram no matter where you are. By discovering your strengths, passions and future market trends, you will be able to craft a series of steps, such as job switches, acquiring new skills, getting an Masters Degree, re-tooling, industry-exits, among others, that will bring you closer to the centre.

If you are already in the centre, then having a coherent Career Strategy will ensure that you remain there.

BONUS MATERIAL

Is it always ideal to be in the middle of the Venn Diagram? Are there other reasons to stay away from the middle? Visit www.career-strategy.com/bonus and key "Venn" to access this extra article.

Chapter 5

Should you stay or leave?

"Should I stay or should I go?
If I go there will be trouble
And if I stay it will be double
So come on and let me know."
—THE CLASH (1981)

Many of us face this question at some time in our career. After years of doing the same job in the same company or industry, you may want to experience a new environment, face new challenges, and of course, get paid more for it. Whether you decide to move on to greener pastures or to stay put, you need to examine your motivation for taking the next step very carefully. Are you moving for the right reasons or are you staying for the wrong ones? This chapter will delve in greater detail, the most common reasons to explore a job change and whether these are valid. The reasons are broadly categorised into environmental and personal.

REAL-LIFE CAREER STORY

Sarah, 42, Teacher

Sarah was at the top her game in her company. She had spent the last eighteen years building her reputation and track record as one of her organisation's Global Top Talent and was known inside and even outside the business as the 'Fixer'.

However, Sarah felt a bit bored with what she did. At 42, she was already a VP in charge of one of their flagship product portfolios and knew the entire industry well. "Sometimes, a bit *too well*," she shared, "I think I may have peaked too soon—there's almost no more opportunities here. I'd like to explore what's outside myw company or industry. Is this a valid reason for me to consider moving?"

Environmental reasons

Your company is being (or has been) acquired

In today's world of mergers and acquisitions, even companies with the healthiest balance sheets could easily become targets for acquisition. Mega-mergers and buy-outs are common in the marketplace and as the saying goes, "When elephants battle, the ants perish."

Often, the main reason for mergers and acquisitions is to establish synergies—corporate-speak for reducing costs by joining forces and removing overlapping functions. Often, this means that one party has to go. Take for instance, the US$7.6 billion acquisition of Nokia by Microsoft in April 2014. It was only a matter of time (three months, as a matter of fact) before Microsoft announced that 18,000 jobs would be cut.

Most mergers and acquisitions are accompanied by retrenchments and those are never in your control. So if you hear rumours of such activities in your industry or company, then keep an eye out for new opportunities in the market.

Your job security is being threatened

Some of us may even see our own roles diminishing in importance or at risk of disappearing altogether. For example, many Chief Information Officer (CIO) roles are being outsourced to faraway places in Asia.

Sometimes, it may not even be your fault that your job becomes uncertain. Your company's US market may have lost a sizeable amount of money and has dragged down global revenues. Even though your region may have been enjoying its second year of record profits, the board may decide to conduct a world wide right-sizing to reduce costs before the next quarter's investors conference call and your job may be on the line.

It could also be caused by something unrelated. The financial crisis of 2008 resulted in many kneejerk reactions that spilled over to non-finance-related industries. Threats to your job exist all the time—it takes great wisdom and far-sightedness to anticipate and plan your exit strategy before it strikes. If the cause is an industry specific one, then you have to think hard about how to exit your sector and plant new roots in a different market.

You foresee that your industry will be in decline soon

In today's fast-changing world, disruptive technologies have been known to put entire companies out of business. Companies like Amazon have almost killed the retail book and Compact Disc selling industries with the ease of online shopping and comparable prices.

A wide range of nightmare scenarios could happen in your business. You realise that the market or product you are serving is fast becoming obsolete. For instance, your company may be involved in older technology that is being replaced by newer, cheaper and better products—such as traditional printed newspapers and magazines being replaced by online publishing and advertising. Or perhaps your industry is in a sunset phase—such as the Yellow Pages, which sells business listings for companies via a voluminous four-inch thick, five-thousand-page directory. Or maybe the market for your product is quickly evaporating—some recruitment firms specialising in entry-level jobs are being replaced by online job portals.

You need to be constantly on the lookout for such trends. We are often caught up in the daily grind of meeting targets and deadlines and may not notice that the industry might not be around in the next five years, and when that happens, would you possess the ability or skills to quickly move to another?

Office politics is getting out of hand

Office politics are a major killjoy at work. In some organisations, the politics can rise to toxic levels, hampering the ability of the teams to perform. We may have heard of or experienced such unhealthy environments. Sometimes, it is caused by just one person, while at other times, it may even be part of the corporate culture. Should the level of politics exceed your threshold for tolerance, it is time to move on for better peace of mind and happiness. This is clearly a valid reason to move.

Personal reasons

You no longer identify with the goals of the organisation

Maybe you have been working at the company for too long and over time, there has been a change in values at the organisation or within yourself. Or there might have been a dramatic shift in the business model, business goal or operations that makes it difficult for you to reconcile with and you feel uncomfortable in the company. Several examples include:

- *Hostile acquisition or friendly merger.* The acquiring organisation may not share your company's vision and culture and may even demand changes to your business processes. One CEO from a small startup firm was shell-shocked to learn that it was being acquired by a large MNC—he described it as "the death-knell for the way we did business."

- *New business ventures or focus.* A client in a strategy consultancy firm was upset that her firm started a 'gaming division' catering exclusively to the casino and gambling industry in Asia. She was even more upset to be tasked to set it up. "I have very strong reservations towards gambling," she confided. Another friend in the accounting industry left his company when it started dealing with tobacco companies for extra revenue—an act he felt was 'unconscionable'.

- *New leader.* Sometimes, a less experienced senior executive is brought in from corporate headquarters in London, New York or Mumbai. Or maybe the CEO of a more aggressive competitor has been hired by the board to initiate change in the organisation. He makes drastic changes to the structure, placing his former colleagues into your team, making 'unreasonable demands' on sales targets, and commences the purging of long-serving employees. These changes can be quite disruptive and will take the joy out of work.

If these scenarios happen to you, you need to ask yourself whether the company has changed—or that it is you who is unable to adapt to a new and evolving marketplace. If your organisation adopts a more aggressive sales strategy, it may be in response to intense competition which is common today. Even if you move to another company, you may face a similar reality there. This is why you really need to examine your motivations and see whether yours is a valid reason or just a convenient excuse.

Travel, responsibilities or hours are affecting your work-life balance and physical and mental health

With most companies focused on emerging markets like China and India, jobs will become more regional or global in nature, which means an increase in travel for many employees. In the long run, this may take a toll on your personal life, family time and perhaps your health.

One candidate who traveled 80 percent of the time to different timezones complained that she would wake up in the middle of the night in her hotel room, wondering which country she was in and had to dial '0' to ask the operator where she was. Another senior executive shared that he could only see his daughter grow longer, and not taller, because she was always fast asleep when he got home.

You may have been appointed additional markets, product-lines or divisions to manage. Though this is a promotion, it could also mean less time for family dinners. While this adds to your career experience, it will take time and focus away from your core activities. It may work fine if we can handle the expanded work scope and develop 'new muscles' in the short term. However, there may come a time when responsibilities grow unreasonably out of hand and spin out of control. If you are in the unfortunate throes of an overworked schedule or have chalked up enough flight miles in the past six months to fly to London and back on business class, now is the time for honest self-evaluation.

Looking for another job may not be the only solution as the next one might require a similar degree of travel, scope or responsibility. Consider other solutions. You could perhaps hire better area managers so you don't have to travel to Bhutan every week, give up the Sierra Leone market on grounds of personal safety or even decline the invitation to spearhead your company's new auditing project in Lhasa. So you may not need to resign. However, if the situation does not improve and there is no way out, this is a legitimate reason for considering a move.

There is no room for career advancement
As a seasoned headhunter, I hear this very often. It leads me to one of two conclusions—that the candidate genuinely has no upward mobility at all; or that he or she isn't good enough to beat the internal competition for the top position.

Either way, it is a valid justification for leaving the company as long as you are being honest with yourself. There is no shame in admitting that you were passed over for a promotion. In 2001, two senior leaders in General Electric, James McNerney and Robert Nardelli were passed over for the CEO role. They both left and McNerney became the CEO of 3M whilst Nardelli went on to become CEO of Home Depot.

Sometimes, the company may be family-owned and unless you share the same last names as the owners, you may never be entrusted with the family jewels. Or maybe the present CEO has no immediate plans to retire or step down in the foreseeable future, so there may never be any chance of taking his place.

Once again, I reiterate that if you honestly feel that there is not going to be an improvement in circumstances that is *not of your own doing*, then this is a valid reason for moving. Otherwise, you will be carrying the same burden over to the next job and will soon face the same issue of career stagnation again.

I hate my boss!

This reason may not sound valid, but unfortunately it does happen. You may have a new boss brought in from another country or from across the hallway. Perhaps he might even be your peer or junior. His style may not fit yours and he may have different expectations. Or maybe, he just hates your guts.

Whatever the reasons (and there could be more than one), irreconcilable differences with your boss can make life terrible. Quitting should not be your first option as you might later find that the problem does not lie with him but with your inability to adapt or your own biases.

My suggestion is for you to be patient and you may even outlast him. You could also sit down and try to reason this with him—understand where he's coming from and try to accommodate this new style of working. He may not be as unreasonable as you think he is.

However, if you do feel that this new arrangement is something you are unable to live with, then it would be a valid reason for moving on. Do make a mental note of this when considering your next role and ensure you do not have to report to a similar personality type again.

You are bored with your job

This happens to the best of us at some point in our career. Something has changed and you now dread going to work in the morning. You feel that running the business offers no further challenges and have stopped enjoying it. It could be because you have mastered the game and feel that there is nothing new to experience and are just cruising along. Or maybe you are just tired of the daily grind performed for the past fifteen years. Whatever the reasons, you sense yourself quickly losing your passion for work and the thought of having to carry on for the next decade in this same fashion is frightening. You want something new and more exciting to keep you energised.

If you are feeling this way, you are in a career rut. But before you make any drastic decisions, you need to ask yourself whether this situation is temporary or permanent. Are you at a seasonal low, waiting for the action to pick up again in the next quarter when your clients are in their purchasing cycle or is there really no light at the end of a very long and dark tunnel? You need to be clear about whether this is a passing phase or just the start of another cycle.

Quitting a job because of a lack of challenge is always a valid reason. As professionals who thrive on new experiences, we always want to learn new things and stay sharp. However, you also need to explore whether there are other ways of making your job more exciting and fun, such as taking on a new project, coaching a new protégé, increasing your portfolio, etc. Changing jobs just because you are bored may not address the problem directly and might lead you to unrealistically take on another job that is overly ambitious with too many challenges, burning you out within months of joining the new organisation.

You're planning a long overdue career change

"I want to see what's out there!"—I get really excited whenever candidates say this. Here's a fine example of someone who is planning his career and open to options that might advance the quality of his life. Sometimes, they want to move into a different company, sometimes, into a different role. Sometimes, they want to jump into something radically different and although it is not impossible, it requires a high degree of strategic thinking and long-term planning. (See Chapter 6 on "Switching Careers: Know your Career Pivots™")

This is always a valid reason to move. But do not to be impulsive—one candidate quit his job to start up a childcare centre (which he had no prior experience in) only to see his investment crash and burn within six months. He simply woke up one morning, submitted his resignation letter to his boss, walked across the street to register the new company and bought over a childcare centre without doing proper homework. Needless to say, the chances for success were slim and he lost his retirement savings on that venture.

Before making a life changing career switch, you need to be aware of the risks. Even in straightforward situations like joining your competitor, you could be hit with a non-competition lawsuit, or worse, the organisation you joined is acquired by your former company and you are once again reporting to your former boss who is not amused by your antics.

My advice is that before you make a long overdue career change, talk to your spouse or family first. Get his or her buy-in and support, highlighting your need for change and how it will positively enhance your family situation. You may also want to ensure you have a relatively healthy bank balance to tide you over just in case the move doesn't work out and you are left without income in between jobs.

Most importantly, think long and hard about where you are headed—you need to make a long-term plan with long-term goals. A well thought-out roadmap will guide you through such uncertainties.

Your life situation has changed

Some things that happen in our lives are beyond our control; perhaps you just got married, had a baby or have had a close relative struck by illness. Whatever the reasons, you may be facing a situation that calls for an urgent and immediate re-evaluation of your career. Your present salary and benefits may no longer be sufficient to support your lifestyle or you may need a lighter workload to free up more time for your personal matters.

If possible, do not leave your job outright. If you are already facing a crisis, leaving your job for a new one might worsen the situation, after all, it has been said that a job change is one of the most stressful events in life. The last thing you need is another traumatic situation to cope with—new colleagues, a new environment, new processes and new responsibilities—all while managing your current crisis. Worse yet, it might even affect your performance at the new job, raising doubts on your abilities.

You might want to consider working out alternative solutions like getting time off, taking temporary no-pay leave, a salary-advance or a sabbatical. However, if this option is not available to you, then you may have to consider taking charge of things and looking for alternative arrangements. In such a situation, a change in working environment would be valid.

Better pay and prestige

A mentor of mine always says, "Money doesn't buy happiness, but it sure does make you feel happy!"

One of the reasons I hear from candidates wanting to leave their job is "I want more money. I deserve more money, I'm being paid below my market rate." It is true that everybody wants more money—that is a basic tenet of man's existence, or as Gordon Gecko (Michael Douglas in the movie *Wall Street*) so eloquently put it, "Greed is good!"

However, what we have to realise is that often, *there is a price to more money*. There are some factors to consider when we talk about salaries. Let me introduce you to the 'Stress/Dollar Factor'.

Stress/Dollar Factor

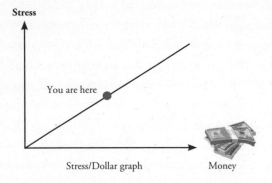

Stress/Dollar graph　　　　　Money

Let the grey dot in the centre of the graph above represent where you currently are in your career; that is, your current remuneration and workload. We will explore the various possible outcomes involved when a change of job and salary happens.

Career Move #1: Status Quo?

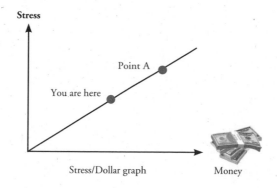

Stress/Dollar graph

If you move to a job that pays better, but has a commensurate increase in difficulty or workload (in the form of a bigger portfolio, more clients, bigger team to manage, increased regional responsibilities), you would be moving to Point A.

Many argue that this constitutes a fair promotion—more pay for more work. However, there would be others who would see it as zero value-add—you are still on what economists call 'The Line of Indifference'. Will such a move enhance your life?

REAL-LIFE CAREER STORY

Susan, 55, Sales Director

Susan is a 55-year-old sales director who was offered a job that increased her salary by half. In return, she had to increase her sales by 50 percent. She is quite happy where she is and feels that as she is only seven years away from retirement, she doesn't need the increase in stress and travel. "I'd rather stay in my current role because any increase in salary is offset by longer hours and more responsibilities. I am indifferent to the new position." Moreover, Susan felt that if she wanted to, she could drive her sales teams harder and put in the additional effort, leading to a 50 percent increase in sales and a similar increase in commissions—all without the additional stress of moving to a new company. So she turned it down.

Career Move #2: Working hard for the money

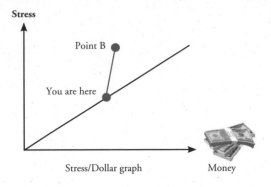

Stress/Dollar graph

Perhaps an exciting role comes along that offers you a 50 percent increase in salary. However, the workload is going to be 100 percent more than your current portfolio.

Is this going to be a wise move? Will you be able to cope with the increased demands or will you feel cheated and resentful, looking back with regret on the days of easy money? How long will you last in the new organisation before you burn out?

REAL-LIFE CAREER STORY

Sarah, Compliance Officer

Sarah, a compliance officer, quit her adequately paid civil service job to join a renowned commodity trading house for a hefty 50 percent increase in salary.

After she joined them, she realised that instead of the nine-to-five culture she was accustomed to, she had to work late almost every day, including weekends, often bringing work home to meet tight deadlines.

"I was paid more, but I was doing the work of three people!" she complained. Needless to say, she soon returned to her previous job, happy to be back in her comfort zone.

Career Move #3: A better deal

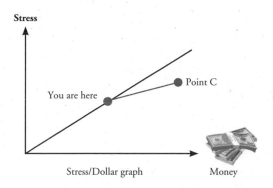

Sometimes, fortune smiles on us and we land an offer where the money is better and relatively speaking, the increase in workload is manageable. Maybe you're moving to a similar role from a small privately-owned company, where the compensation isn't as exciting, to a MNC with a healthier budget for salaries.

So which career move do I choose?

The strategy you choose largely depends on which phase of life you are in. As an aspiring young go-getter in the early years of your career, you can afford to be bold—choose Career Moves #1 or #2. The increased exposure will be good for your career and you still have the energy and drive to manage the new challenges.

But this path may not be suitable for someone in their late-forties, where money may not be the key driving factor for career decisions. Other considerations like family and health may take priority, hence Career Move #3 would be a good option.

In general, we always need to consider the money when we move but it must *never* be the sole reason for moving. Many candidates who have made the foolish decision to leave their jobs just because the money was more attractive later realised that the new role or company was not suitable. So we should be aware of the Stress/Dollar Factor—any move that shifts you above the line of indifference must be considered carefully—are you ready to put in more effort than might be worth?

Any move along that line brings more money but is accompanied by a similar increase in responsibilities. Does that bode well for you at this point in your life? Maybe you don't need the money and prefer to spend more time with your family. Or perhaps you *do* need the extra cash and won't mind working harder and longer. No one has the right answer for you except yourself. Use this tool to frame the deal you are looking at and draw your own conclusions.

Career Move #4: Taking your foot off the accelerator

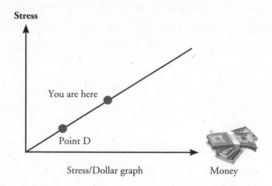

Some candidates always joke about Career Move #4. They feel that it might be an acceptable option to go for a reduced pay for a reduced salary package to slow down. They do not even mind if that means a demotion in rank from regional director to sales manager if it means a lighter workload.

Whilst some may flinch at the idea of taking home less money, others may welcome the thought of having better work-life balance, especially when they don't really need that much money.

REAL-LIFE CAREER STORY

Winnie, Regional HR Vice-president

Winnie, a regional HR vice-president with an annual salary of over US$300,000 a year decided that her hectic travel schedule and almost nightly conference calls to the US was too much to bear. She had over 2,000 employees to account for and was getting very tired. She confessed of her desire to slow down and wasn't too worried about the money as her husband was a surgeon.

Coincidentally, another client, a European chemicals company was looking for an HR Manager to run a newly set-up local plant with less than sixty employees on site. I introduced them—he felt that he was getting the best deal and Winnie was delighted with the nine-to-five working hours that came with the job. She did not mind that it was slightly less than half her previous salary, saying, "After all, US$140,000 a year is still more than what I really need."

BONUS MATERIAL

Now you have the right reasons for leaving—how about the six wrong reasons for staying in your job? Login to www.career-strategy.com/bonus and key "wrong" to access this extra article.

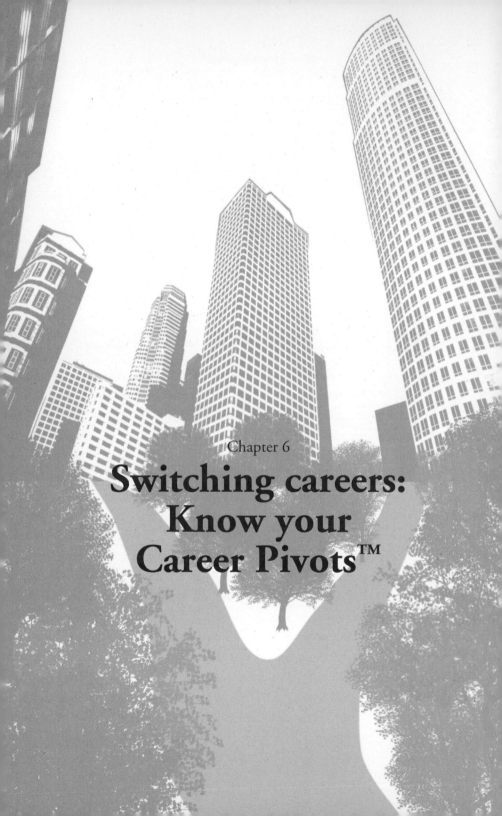

Chapter 6

Switching careers:
Know your
Career Pivots™

Debbie sat at her desk, staring blankly at the back of the class as her rowdy students bounced off each other like energised atoms in a nuclear reactor about to detonate. Just a year ago, she was a high-flying lawyer who had it all—a good salary, a company car, and even a personal assistant. But today, it was crowd control ... no ... zoo-keeping would be a better description for her job. Suddenly, the unreasonable demands from corporate clients and all-nighters spent preparing impossible-to-win cases seems like a walk in the park compared to handling a motley group of over-privileged kids. "At least I was being paid better for the amount of effort I put in at the old job!"

Debbie was a client who sought my career-coaching services. As a trained lawyer, she had worked fifteen years in prestigious law firms and had a sterling career. However, she felt frustrated at her workplace and decided to make a career switch. She decided one morning to quit and become a teacher.

"Teaching—how tough could that be?" She thought. She resigned that day and signed up with the National Education Board to be trained as a teacher. The first year of training was fun as it was light and easy. But once she graduated and was posted to one of the top schools in the country, she suddenly realised that she had no passion for teaching at all. Long hours spent correcting her students' work and administering forms was absolutely boring for her.

"I had no idea it was this mundane and stressful. I really wished I thought harder about this switch and looked for something more in line with my strengths and passion. Perhaps I was a bit too hasty and naive. Maybe I should sign up for a course at Le Cordon Bleu and become a pastry chef instead!"

So, you have decided that it's time to leave your current job for a more attractive one. You are considering reinventing yourself and jumping into a different but more exciting industry. Whatever the case may be, bear in mind that career-switches are never risk-free, so remember one key point.

DON'T BE HASTY!

I have seen many candidates and friends get so frustrated with their work/boss/colleagues that they quit their jobs to take on something totally unrelated to their background and training. Or worse still, like Debbie, take on a role that is incongruent with their temperaments. Some executives even quit with no job in hand, expecting to get another role within the next month or two before realising that the job market is a lot tougher than before and especially unkind towards older employees. Very often, it is the beginning of downward spiral for them and it takes some time for them to find their footing again.

Everything starts with a plan

For many of us, the ideal next job could be one that's similar to what we are doing today, except perhaps with a little more scope, responsibility and hopefully, pay. For example, a sales director could look forward to becoming a Managing Director with a competitor. If only things could always be as simple and straightforward all the time.

However, some executives may not want to remain in the same industry or function in their next move. Reasons would include, "I don't want to join a competitor" to "this particular role is not exciting anymore."

For various reasons, we may want to make a total career switch for a complete change of environment. Some senior managers may have been at the top of their game for a long time and have grown bored with their industry or role.

Andrew, a senior vice-president in his mid-forties, told me that after twenty years in the pharmaceutical sector, he had learnt everything he could about it and had lost his passion for the business.

Another sales director in the contract manufacturing sector, William, shared with me that the writing was on the wall—his industry was in decline as most of the business had gone to low-cost countries like China and Vietnam. So he had to look for a total switch in industry or he would not have a job for long.

Others may have discovered that there has to be more to life than work and wished to explore how their strengths could be leveraged to another industry.

Whatever the reasons may be, these people want to make a career switch but are unsure or even afraid of doing so. In response to this, I have developed a step-by-step framework to manage this process, called the *Career PLAN*.

Making a complete switch into a role or industry that you have absolutely no clue about could lead to career suicide. Like a mountain-climber scaling a treacherous vertical cliff, you need to have at least one hand or foot firmly anchored to the wall before you pivot yourself upwards, making sure that it is a strong one with a solid grip.

Likewise, you need at least one *Career Pivot* to firmly attach yourself to the new role in order to make your move a smooth and successful one. Let me elaborate further.

Your Career PLAN™

In order to facilitate a smooth transition from one role or function and industry to another, you must have at least one Career Pivot. Examples of Career Pivots could be your sales management expertise, your specific industry knowledge, your particular skillsets, or even your charm and influence with people.

A CAREER PIVOT IS A SPECIFIC ATTRIBUTE YOU POSSESS (AND EXCEL) IN YOUR CURRENT JOB THAT CAN BE QUICKLY AND EFFECTIVELY APPLIED IN YOUR *NEXT* JOB.

By leveraging on these attributes, transitioning and excelling in the next role will be much easier. These Career Pivots can be into four groups:

- Your **P**assion
- Your **L**earning
- Your **A**ptitude
- Your **N**etwork

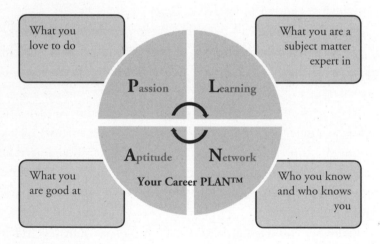

Know your passion

What does Steve Jobs, Richard Branson, Bill Gates and Elon Musk have in common (besides a few billion dollars in their bank account)?

Passion.

Steve Jobs always had a passion for good design and Richard Branson would never invest in any business he wasn't passionate about.

Passion is the fuel that drives people and if you are able to identify and tap into this resource, you will really enjoy what you are doing. You need to look deep into yourself to find out what excites you. What puts that spring in your step every morning? What can you go on talking about without getting tired?

My mentor once said, "If you are a nurse and your child asks you what you do for a living, don't tell him 'I'm a nurse'. Tell him, 'I'm the person who's going to help people feel better today!' If you are an accountant, do not respond with 'I stare at numbers all day' but tell him 'I help my company make the right decisions!'"

How we view our work often determines the way we feel about our jobs. We need to find out what we are most passionate about. We can then use this passion as a pivot into the possible options in our next career.

For example, consider Khoo Swee Chiow, Singapore's most famous adventurer and a good friend. He is very passionate about trekking and started a professional adventure tours company, bringing the bravest souls as far as to Mount Everest and K2 for a fee. To him, work is pleasure and he gets to do what he loves every day. (Read more about his Career Story at the end of this chapter.)

I have always been passionate about career counseling, often being invited by educational institutions to give talks on career guidance to students. It was this passion that drove me to leave a high-flying job with GE Plastics towards a career in headhunting over a decade ago. Being in executive search, I am able to coach my candidates on a daily basis and be exposed to a field that I am most passionate about. As a result, I have enjoyed every moment of my career and am still energised after all these years.

Ask yourself, "What really excites me? What would I do for free? What makes me truly happy? What hobbies do I have?

If I didn't have to worry about bills to pay, what would I be doing all day?" It could be coaching, it could be working with children or it could even be cooking.

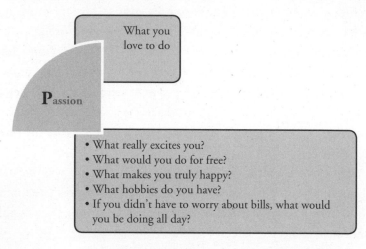

Knowing what excites you and what non-work-related areas of your life you are probably really good at could give you an insight into an alternative, out-of-the-box idea about industries or business ideas you could explore further. You may not have the network or know-how but because you are really interested in it, your learning curve and transition will be a lot smoother.

Know your learning

After many years in your industry, there are some very specific processes, markets or regulations that you should know very well. You could be the subject matter expert in terms of supply-chain management, how to streamline a manufacturing process or how to save the company money by simply restructuring their finances offshore (legally).

This knowledge can be categorised into functional knowledge or domain (industry) knowledge, as illustrated next.

What you are a subject matter expert in

Learning

Functional knowledge
Examples:
- Managing a team of scientists
- Sales training
- Financial accounting, HR, etc
- Negotiating complex deals
- Navigating complex regulatory requirements
- Selling highly technical products

Domain (industry) knowledge
Examples:
- Understanding how your oil trading/pharmaceutical/electronics market works
- Knowing the retail food and beverage industry
- Understanding the damand and supply behaviour of consumers in your sector
- Understanding the particular trends and quirks of your market

Functional knowledge—Knowing the specifics of your job

Functional knowledge is your deep understanding of the job you have been in. It could be knowing how to negotiate complex merger deals or navigating complicated regulatory requirements with the local authorities. It is information that not many others outside your department or business may possess and even if they did, would not be able to do it was well as you.

Maybe you know how to package products to sell to high-networth individuals, or perhaps migrating legacy computer systems to modern day platforms. These are examples of functional knowledge you have collected and mastered over the years.

Can you name three of yours?

One candidate, Angela, was a sales director in the insurance industry specialising in developing high performance sales teams. She had a very strong understanding of the lead generation and sales management process, most of which she had developed for her team. This knowledge was highly valued by a real estate sales company who wanted to improve their sales processes to boost sales, so I headhunted her to be their regional sales effectiveness director.

Another candidate, Robin, a credit card marketing manager had inside knowledge of how to drive membership and usage of her bank's credit cards. She knew how to manage a large database of users and apply data-analytics to ensure they were kept engaged and loyal to the brand, thus spending more money with them. My client, a US-based Fast Moving Consumer Goods (FMCG) company wanted to embark on a customer relationship management program and found that her knowledge was highly relevant, even though she was from a totally different industry.

Sometimes, you do not even need to know everything about your particular business. Sometimes, just the narrow sliver of the most critical parts would do. For instance, instead of knowing everything about the aviation industry, simply mastering the last minute pricing strategy of airline seats may put you in a good demand from online hotel booking sites.

Domain knowledge—Knowing the specifics of your industry

Domain or industry knowledge consist of the very technical bits of information that may be industry- or company-specific. Because you have many years of experience in your industry, you could be the person who owns all this knowledge and have become the expert in this area. In today's knowledge-based economy, this is gold. Companies will hire you for knowing what to do and how to do it, and the deeper your knowledge, the more valuable you could be to them. This technical expertise could make you very attractive to a competitor or even to another company who is from a completely different industry as you, but needing the same skillsets. For example, a bank's call centre expert can still be hired by a mobile phone company wanting to set up a customer support call centre.

As a Career Pivot, domain knowledge or functional knowledge is the key to allow you to migrate to a different sector or role. Having a big picture understanding of your industry often gives you a greater advantage in terms of transferability.

REAL-LIFE CAREER STORIES

Tom, Operations Director

Tom was the operations director at a major oil company. In his twenty-year career, he had worked in the top five oil companies and wanted to switch to something different. Because of his deep understanding of the needs and requirements of the major oil companies and broad knowledge of challenges and market trends in this sector, I headhunted him into an oilfield equipment company as their sales director. Although he did not have the sales experience, he managed to impress his clients with his in-depth technical knowledge and could close more deals than his sales-focused predecessors. His industry knowledge was transferable across companies.

Sarah, Regional Sales and Marketing Director

Sarah was a regional sales and marketing director in a drug company. Having spent fifteen years in this industry, she accumulated vast knowledge of the business in the region and their peculiarities. Feeling bored with sales, she switched to a purely HR role and became her company's HR director. Because of her deep understanding of the business and solid reputation in the market, the switch was successful as she was willing to learn and reinvent herself.

Knowing what your domain or functional knowledge is could be your *greatest asset* in your search for a new career.

With an understanding of how your knowledge could be a strength or a shortcoming, you will be able to formulate your Career Strategy and provide clarity towards the direction you are heading.

When you are leveraging on your Learning, there are basically four types of career moves you can make. The table below frames the four options you have.

	Same functional knowledge	Different functional knowledge
Same domain/ industry knowledge	**Ideal** Easiest to switch over (Eg. Finance manager from an oil company to finance manager for another oil company) **STRATEGY A**	**Possible** Need to be versatile and have very strong domain knowledge (Eg. Finance manager from an oil company to HR manager for another oil company) **STRATEGY C**
Different domain/ industry knowledge	**Easier** Core skills are already on hand, just need to learn peculiarities of the new industry (Eg. Finance manager from an oil company to finance manager for an IT company) **STRATEGY B**	**Challenging** Steep learning curve and employers may not give you that opportunity—need other Career Pivots to be strong (Eg. Finance manager from an oil company to HR manager for an IT company) **STRATEGY D**

Career moves leveraging on your functional/domain knowledge:

- *Strategy A.* Ideally, a switch of company in the same role and industry is a straightforward move. But in terms of excitement and career progression, is this going to be more of the same? Will you be bored after a while?
- *Strategy B.* The second easier option is moving into a different industry but retaining the same function and role. However, be prepared to embark on a steeper learning curve. This move may not be available to all as their functional knowledge may be specific to the industry—a drug company's regulatory director may have deep but highly specific knowledge about the pharmaceutical market that is not easily transferred to other industries.
- *Strategy C.* The third way would be moving into a different role in a similar industry. For a move like this, you need to have very strong fundamental industry knowledge. A good market reputation also helps, and having a 'sponsor' in the new company, someone willing to take a chance on you, increases your likelihood of success. However, you need to move quickly into learning mode and realise that there will be a huge degree of retooling necessary.
- *Strategy D.* The final and most challenging pathway is the fish-out-of-water move. I generally discourage different role and industry moves as there are just too many variables. However, if your other Career Pivots are strong—Passion, Aptitude and Networks—and you can leverage on as many as possible, then you will have a better chance of succeeding with a move like this.

Know your aptitude

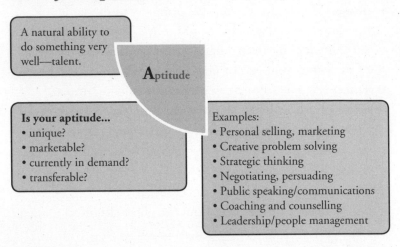

A natural ability to do something very well—talent.

Aptitude

Is your aptitude...
- unique?
- marketable?
- currently in demand?
- transferable?

Examples:
- Personal selling, marketing
- Creative problem solving
- Strategic thinking
- Negotiating, persuading
- Public speaking/communications
- Coaching and counselling
- Leadership/people management

What skills have you picked up in your years working? It is good to have a long list of skills, but what are you *really* great at? Everyone can say they have sales leadership skills, but how many can proudly say that under their guidance, their sales teams have tripled revenues in less than a year?

When discussing the Career Strategy, we do not want to just talk about *skills.* We want to frame our abilities in terms of aptitude—which is talent or the natural ability to do something very well. There are three key elements that determine how far you can leverage it in your search for a new career:

- *Is it unique?* Is your talent rare in the market or is it commoditised? Being able to explain complex financial concepts in layman terms is a skill that many tax accountants may lack, so those who can are well paid for it. Being able to program efficiently in C++ may be your forte but can this ability be purchased at a cheaper rate? Focus your aptitude on unique strengths and you will stand out from the crowd.

- *Is it marketable and currently in demand?* So what if you can yodel while playing the accordion? Having a talent that is not marketable will get you nowhere. Is your talent in great demand? Are you able to design a new type of memory chip or manage a multi-million-dollar project within a tight budget and deadline? The more unique your talent is, the more the employer will pay for it. But note that some talent have a shelf-life. There was a very strong demand for people with business analytics knowledge in 2003 to 2007, as the market for such business intelligence software companies like Cognos, Hyperion and Business Objects grew rapidly. But by late 2010, these once favoured companies were acquired by software giants like SAP, Oracle and IBM, and demand for these areas faltered. Ironically, with the return of Big Data (the software industry's latest darling catchphrase about utilising data to increase revenues) today, the demand for such skills is picking up once again.

- *Is it transferable?* Talents are more useful if they are transferable. Being able to sell a car and only a car isn't going to be very useful to someone who wants to break out of his industry. However, being able to coach and lead teams in various scenarios and situations would be a very desirable skill to possess, whatever the industry. Trying to be a 'Jack of all trades, master of some' helps widen your career options because it allows you to be versatile with a wide range of skills to tap into. Being able to identify transferable skills is critical for your career transition. It acts as the bridge from one industry to another. For instance, having a finance manager background enables one to easily move between sectors. Alternatively, a marketing person who organises a lot of launch events could join an events company as their sales or operations manager. Another example could be a consumer insights manager for a fast moving consumer goods company joining a consumer behaviour research company, or vice versa. Having a highly marketable and transferable skill increases your demand in the market, broadening your options considerably.

Here are a list of talent that employers are looking for:
- Personal selling
- Marketing
- Creative problem solving
- Strategic thinking
- Negotiating and persuading
- Public speaking and communications
- Coaching/counselling
- Leadership
- People management
- Project management
- Writing
- Research and planning

Usually, the outward sign of possessing a talent is not in saying that you have it but displayed with a proven track record. If you have a history of managing projects successfully, then this is probably your talent.

How do I discover my strengths?

Many of us struggle to identify what we are really good at and often take the tasks we do well for granted. However, there are some good ideas of drawing up a possible list of strengths. Ask yourself: What am I really good at? Have people complimented me on any particular ability? What was my proudest achievement and what did I do so well to make it happen?

Another more structured way is for you to take a psychometric test like the Harrison Assessment (available at www.career-strategy.com) or read *Strengths Finder 2.0*, written by Tom Rath. These guides will help you to better understand your natural talents and what you find may even surprise you.

Know your network

One aspect of our professional life that we often ignore is our network. In today's interconnected world, we are unlikely to be operating in isolation. Every contact is a potential point for future reference. As we consider new career options, we need to be able to identify and leverage on our existing networks, and perhaps monetise them. Our network system could be summarised in the following diagram.

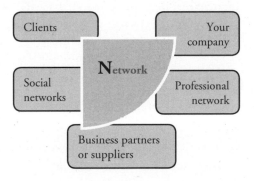

Clients

The vast network of clients you serve in your industry represents a rich source of potential opportunities. If you have been servicing them well and have a good reputation or standing with them, you could join a competitor and sell your new products or services to them. Better still, you could even join your client. One candidate, Ivy, was a sales manager in the pharmaceutical sector who sold products mainly to surgeons and medical doctors. She decided to exit the industry in 2006 to become a real estate sales agent and began to sell to her existing clients, who already knew her well. She was an overnight success as until then, these highly paid medical professionals did not have an agent they trusted. Suddenly, she was leveraging on her network and trusted reputation to make recommendations on property investments. Today, Ivy is running her own successful agency.

Social networks

These do not just include contacts on online social networks but also friends and fellow enthusiasts who share a common hobby or interest. One candidate, Lilian, decided to transform her hobby of online shopping into a respectable spree-buying business (making bulk purchases online for large groups of people). By aggregating her entire list of friends and contacts, she was able to form a much larger group, which increased their purchasing power.

Professional network

This group includes your present and past colleagues and even industry peers from rival companies. Because your reputation and experience in your domain is so strong, you could leverage yourself as an expert resource or consultant to the business. A former client, Clarence, was a very successful insurance sales manager who retired in his early fifties and conducts sales training workshops for young agents of companies he used to compete against. By targeting his professional network of fellow insurance salespeople, he has a ready niche of potential clients waiting to learn from the best in the industry.

Your company

Sometimes, the company we work for could be our strongest network waiting to be tapped. Who would be better placed to understand the needs and requirements of one's own company? A friend, Leonard, was operations director of a very large global logistics company who after eighteen years of working with them, had inside knowledge of the complexities, requirements and politics peculiar to his organisation's structure. He knew the challenges and types of people needed to resolve them. Wanting a change of career, he joined a top executive search firm and his first (and only) client has been his former company who was all-to-pleased to have an insider who understood the work culture and could identify top talents for them. Selling to your own company seems obvious but is often overlooked.

Business partners or suppliers

Another huge network to be tapped would be your suppliers or business partners. Because of your long-term relationship with them, you would have already established a certain rapport. Moreover, as you are in the same industry, you understand their challenges well and can add a different perspective to their business. A possible career move could be transitioning from the buy-side to the sell-side. Jeremy, an IT manager from an MNC, whose job was engaging third-party services from a vendor, decided to move into a sales or operations role for that vendor as he would know how MNCs procure that type of service. "It's the same business, just on the opposite end of the negotiation table," he shared.

There have been similar stories of executives who have been poached by their suppliers—it all depends on how well you network with them and also how good your reputation is in the industry. Your network could be very valuable for the next employer or for starting a business. You just need to spend some time thinking about the people you regularly interact with, and the type of opportunities you could leverage from them. In order to get the most out of your networks, remember that they will only want to partner with you if you have been doing a great job working with them, so keep up the good work and watch your network capital grow.

BONUS MATERIAL

To read some true stories of people who successfully switched over into different careers, visit www.career-strategy.com/bonus and key in "pivot" to read more!

REAL-LIFE CAREER STORY

Khoo Swee Chiow, Adventurer

He has trekked to the North and South Poles and has climbed Mount Everest three times. In 2014, he reached the summit of K2, the savage mountain known for taking the life of one out of every four climbers who has attempted to conquer her. He has the honour of being the fourth person in the world to have completed the Explorer's Grand Slam.

His name is Khoo Swee Chiow and he is a full-time adventurer. Who would believe that only fifteen years ago, he was a computer programmer?

It all began in 1987 when he graduated with a computer science degree. He worked with several companies, helping them to build IT systems and solutions, but always retained his passion for the great outdoors. He would do something exciting whenever he travelled for business—from trekking in New Zealand to rock-climbing in the US.

In 1998, Swee Chiow dared to dream big—he wanted to climb Mount Everest. No one in Singapore had done it then and it was unheard of at that time. He started training hard and together with his team, made it to the summit, The following year, he skied to the South Pole, covering a distance of 1,125km in 57 days. He was always excited about these adventures and enjoyed every moment of it.

In 2000, he told his wife that he would be taking a one-year sabbatical leave to try being a full-time adventurer. She supported the idea and at age 36, Swee Chiow put his career on hold to follow his dream. That year, he became the first Southeast Asian to scale the Seven Summits. It wasn't easy as he had to worry about his financial future.

"I was afraid, but I realised that if I do what I'm most passionate about and do it exceptionally well, I will learn new skills. And if I apply those skills exceptionally well, people will be willing to pay me for those skills."

So in 2002, having worked in the IT division for Singapore Airlines for six years, he officially ended his sabbatical by resigning. "It was not an overnight decision but rather, a two-year thinking process."

Swee Chiow started his adventure company, Dare to Dream (www.daretodream.com.sg) and conducts motivational talks and adventure trips to exciting places around the world. He has been very successful in his business and is a role model for many.

I asked what he would have done differently if he had a time machine and he said, "I would have started earlier!" I also asked him what career advice he would give to someone at the second career crossroad and he shared the following:

- *Ignore the 'Nay-sayers'.* There will always be people who will tell you what you want to achieve cannot be done or that it is a dumb idea. Always believe in yourself and you will succeed. Don't let them slow you down.
- *Dream big, but start small.* You don't have to start with a Big Bang—in fact, it might even be very risky to do so. Waiting to gain enough resources to launch that Big Bang may also cause delays and give you cold feet. Test the waters first—you could start by trying out your ideas on a small scale or take a sabbatical to give that idea a shot. Learn from these lessons then decide whether you want to scale the idea upwards.
- *Do!* Don't just talk about it or keep analysing. Take the first step as it is often the scariest, but once you are in it, things will get going. The problem with mid-career changes is that people often think of the money first—Will I earn enough? Will people buy my services?—and the fear stops them from taking action. This is the wrong approach. Once you have a plan, take action.
- *Get out of your comfort zone.* Many times, we do not realise that we are in our comfort zone. We need to move into our discomfort zone and push ourselves harder to grow. It is challenging and difficult but we will develop new muscles that make us stronger.

I asked Swee Chiow what he was most proud of and he shared, "I'm proud that I stayed true to myself and my calling, and do what I really love. I'm also happy that I had a vision and dared to quit my job to follow it."

Today at fifty, he is still planning to take on bigger challenges ahead and will be revisiting K2. I asked him what's next for him and he said, "There's no slowing down! I have another nine 8,000m-peaks to go!"

Swee Chiow is the embodiment of someone who leveraged his Passion (for adventure) and his Aptitude (his leadership and organisational skills) to pivot into another role when he was facing his career crossroad. As the saying 'Fortune favours the bold' goes, indeed, he is enviously living his dream today.

In summary, if you decide to switch career or industry, you will definitely need a strategy. Knowing your various Career Pivots in your PLAN—passion, learning, aptitude and network—will help you to make the switch less painful.

Chapter 7

Landing your
dream job

A memorable sketch from the classic *Monty Python* series is called "Vocational Guidance Counsellor"—it starts off with a young John Cleese as a career coach advising Michael Palin, who plays a chartered accountant, about his career.

After countless interviews and aptitude tests, John Cleese tells him that the ideal job for him was ironically, "Chartered Accountancy." However, Michael Palin refuses to accept that, saying that he knew what his dream job would be—a lion tamer!

"But do you have any qualifications?"

"Yes, a hat! A lion-taming hat that I just bought from Harrods," he replied. "I don't have any experience with lions, but I've seen them at the zoo. They're little brown furry things with short stumpy legs and long noses and they eat ants."

"That's an ant-eater, not a lion!" John Cleese exclaims, "A lion is a huge savage beast with masses of sharp pointed teeth and nasty razor-sharp claws that can rip your belly open before you can say 'Eric Robinson' and they look like this!" He then produces large picture of a lion and shows it to Michael Palin who screams and passes out.

Unlike the character in the sketch, you now have a clearer idea of what role you want to be in and have probably decided in which industry as well. If you have been following the previous chapters, you would now have both a Career Strategy and a Career PLAN to work with.

Job search strategy

As a headhunter, the most frustrating types of calls come from unsolicited jobseekers who ask, "Can you find me a job? I'm good at everything because I am flexible and I can join any industry because I am adaptable. I don't know what I want but I'm sure you can find me a great job!"

The headhunter has no idea what job is best for you, so the key responsibility of the job search lies with you and no one else. The headhunter will never know your industry or profile as well as you do, so take charge and take action!

To find your dream job, you need to develop a job search strategy. As in all business plans, success depends on execution, and in this case, it is going to be the most arduous and lengthy one that requires a lot of patience and tenacity.

Finding a dream job is a job in itself. It requires strategy, time, effort and a lot of research and legwork. It is a journey, not a destination and it will take time. The more senior you are, the longer it may take.

From experience, the job search process may take anywhere from three months (if you are lucky) to a year, so please do not be impatient as there are many variables that are out of your control and there is no way to rush them. Older or more senior candidates may take longer as the market is smaller for them.

Often, executives get impatient and fatigued after just two months and grab whatever job is available out of frustration, regardless of whether it is in line with their Career Strategy or not. This is risky move.

Developing your job search strategy

Step 1: Understand your dream job

Having developed your Career Strategy based on your strengths, what you like doing, your passions, skills and prevailing market trends, you should have already defined your dream job.

It could be the same role that you are in right now but in a different industry, or it could a different role in the same industry. It could also be a total crossover into something you have never tried, into a new role in a new industry. For instance, you may have decided to leave your loans officer role in a bank to search for a sales job with the latest and fastest growing online social network company because it is a growth industry and you are passionate about it.

There is a need to be realistic regarding what you can and cannot do. I would like to be a fighter pilot but am too old for that now. But don't leave idealism out of the equation. Some people have successfully made radical but carefully calculated mid-career switches regardless of their age.

The next step would be to conduct your research. Is the industry you wish to target available in your part of the world? Many executives want to switch to the Green Movement and take part in the renewable energy market, but how many wind turbine companies are based in Singapore? (Only three.)

Do you know anyone in that particular sector, or have you spoken to anyone who is presently in that coveted role? What are his/her opinions about the job—the good, the bad, and the ugly parts? You need to do as much homework as possible so that you know what you are getting yourself into.

Step 2: Make a plan

Charging all out at the market without a strategy in hand is often futile and unsustainable. There needs to be a coherent strategy towards your job search for it to be successful.

Do you have the skills and temperament required?

Having narrowed several roles in key industries, you need to develop a structured approach. Based on your research, you need to find out what particular skills are needed for the target job and whether you have them. What expertise is required to execute that role effectively? More importantly, do you have the temperament to enjoy and excel in the role?

For example, maybe you would like to switch to teaching as profession—do you have the necessary qualifications? Is your degree from a university recognised by the Education Board? Do you have the patience and temperament to be a good teacher? Do you even like children?

If you do not already possess the skills required for the role, can you obtain them? If being a stand-up corporate trainer requires public speaking experience that you do not have, how do you acquire this expertise? Do you join a local toastmaster's club? If being a private banker calls for a huge rolodex of rich people, who do you need to network with to tap into this market? Is this job so different from your current footprint that you need to re-tool and learn an entirely new set of skills? How long would it take to re-train and re-equip for this role?

Create a target list

Now that you know which industry to target, do you know which companies to approach? Are you able to list the top eight companies that you would love to work for and rank them according to preference? This is important because you want to ensure good coverage and that all opportunities are explored.

Having the list is not enough. You need to know who in the organisation you need to approach. Do you send your CV to the HR director or do you email it to your friend working there, requesting that he forwards it to his boss? Do you target your equivalent-rank counterpart there or do you reach out to his supervisor, or should you speak to his supervisor's boss?

This 'targeted' approach is necessary because you need to know who exactly the decision-maker or influencer is. If you are already the vice president of sales, sending a 'please-hire-me letter' to the target company's sales director will get you nowhere as he would think you were after his job. A better strategy would be speaking to the CEO or global vice-president of sales based in their headquarters in the US or Europe, as such high-level decisions are often made at the C-suite.

My advice is to develop several channels of penetration— target multiple entry-points—through HR, through sales, through friends in the company, etc. This vastly increases your chances of a successful hit.

Additionally, you might also want to target headhunters who cover your particular sector. The best headhunters to speak to are those you may have engaged in your career to conduct searches for you. They will be very familiar with your industry and probably owe you a favour or two. Moreover, they would be happy to place a regular into their client's organisation rather than some outsider who may not use their company's services in the future.

Besides companies and headhunters, you should also list your own networks and contacts of ex-bosses, former colleagues, or industry peers that you may have met at various trade shows or conventions. When properly harvested, these could be a rich source of opportunities.

Determine your Value Proposition to the target company
Simply knowing who to target is not enough either. You need to develop a pitch that will get them interested to speak to you. Perhaps Company A has been unable to launch their product into

Indonesia and you have years of experience in that market—I am certain their regional sales director would be happy to have a conversation with you. How could you bring value to their operations? Can you put up a strong business case for hiring you? Would you dare to put a Return on Investment (ROI) figure on your own hiring—how much benefit they can derive by hiring you?

Step 3: Take action

The best laid plans are useless if not executed correctly or if not at all. Now that you have a blueprint for getting that dream job, it is time to launch your very own marketing campaign.

- *Have your resume and online profile ready.* Once you get traction with a contact, you almost immediately need to send your CV over or even be prepared to be searched for online. Ensure your CV is ready and your online profiles, such as LinkedIn, are updated.
- *Adopt a systematic approach.* Go down the list of target companies one by one and keep track of your progress. The best practice is to first send a polite email to the person (such as the CEO, HR director, etc) with a brief introduction and how you can help them solve a particular problem. Then follow up with a phone call three days later to connect with them and check if they have received it. There are three key objectives of the call—to find out if there is a current opening, to find out who the decision maker is, and to secure a meeting. *Remember, your primary goal at this stage is to not to get hired on the spot, but to get a face-to-face meeting, so offer up reasons to meet.* This could be an "I understand you are trying to penetrate the Indonesian Market and I would be happy to share some pitfalls we

made during our market entry three years ago" or even a "I would love to hear your strategic plans for the region and we can exchange some ideas." You don't have to go around, hat-in-hand begging, "Please give me a job, Guv'nor!"

- *Be prepared to get creative.* During the job search, keep an open mind all the time. The opportunity may not come in the exact form that you expected so be very flexible. Instead of a direct job offer, it could be in the form of a one-year contract or even a project-based consultancy arrangement. It could also be an alternative role that could be a bit lower in scope and salary than what you were expecting, but if it gets you a toehold into that much desired company or industry, then it might actually be worth it.

- *Spread the word.* Unless you wish to conduct the job search in absolute secrecy (whatever your reasons may be), it may be a good idea to selectively let your peers know that you are open to career moves. These peers could either be within your company (close friends only, so word does not leak to your boss), or even to your friends or counterparts in the industry. This network could be your very effective 'eyes and ears' in the job marketplace. As a headhunter, prospective candidates who may not be interested in the role usually offer up names of his friends who might be keen. These leads often point me to the best talents available in the market. Having a network of buddies in the market increases your exposure significantly for no extra cost, except perhaps for a cup of coffee or two.

- *Leverage technology.* Use LinkedIn and use it excessively. It is an excellent platform to market yourself and be connected with your target companies and entry-points. Do not forget to include keywords that highlight your special skills and abilities that would flag you up once the recruiter types it in as a search parameters. Do not, however, use Facebook or other social media. It is simply too informal and the pictures and comments may even hurt your professional image.

- *Be resilient and keep trying.* As the saying goes, 'To find that prince, you need to kiss a lot of frogs'. Searching for a job take time and patience, and doors will always slam in your face. Just remember the people who helped you along the way (and the ones who didn't). Someday, you might be able to return the favour.

BONUS MATERIAL

Visit www.career-strategy.com/bonus and key in "dreams" to find out what the three most powerful online strategies to get that dream job are.

Chapter 8
Writing an impactful resume

There are a many books and websites to help you to write the most amazing resume. You will certainly find these articles enlightening, so I shall not re-invent the wheel here but share my inside knowledge as a seasoned resume-reading headhunter.

I have ploughed through more than twenty thousand resumes in my job—these range from the most amusing (a hardcopy sent to me on luminescent pink paper) to the most frightful (twenty-seven-pages long, including appendices).

An HR manager or headhunter gets at least fifty resumes a day and we often do not have time to read every one in detail. The candidate has at most fifteen seconds to pique our interest, and luminescent pink paper does not always do the job.

So, what is the best way to get our attention?

Purpose of a resume

The resume qualifies you for the role and determines whether or not the hiring manager feels it is worth investing over an hour speaking to you face-to-face.

> ALWAYS REMEMBER, THE MAIN PURPOSE OF ANY RESUME
> IS TO WIN YOU THAT FIRST INTERVIEW.

If your resume is unable to interest the reader by conveying how your strengths and achievements can be leveraged to help the hiring company, it will be put face-down into the KIV pile.

Five key pieces of information

Given the sheer amount of data each candidate tries to squeeze into the CV, recruiters have almost no time to study the entire document. Instead, experienced headhunters will qualify each candidate based on a set of parameters to filter out unsuitable applicants.

We typically look for five things before determining whether a particular candidate is viable, so make sure your resume has sufficient relevant information in these five areas and you will be in good stead.

Looking for	Reason
Current position or job title	This piece of information will quickly determine whether you are relevant for the open position. Do you have the right skillsets for the job? Are you are too junior or senior for the role?
Current company	Are you from a competitor or a similar-sized company? Most hiring managers prefer candidates from 'branded' companies (market leaders) as these candidates have been well-trained and (presumably) understand what it takes to win at their game. Alternatively, some companies have a very different culture and may not be a good fit to the hiring company's way of working. So having the wrong pedigree could also hurt your chances.
Duration	Have you been on the job long enough to have made a difference? A candidate who has been a sales director for only nine months (after five years as a sales manager) may be less suitable than another who has been the sales director for four years. Usually, a good time-frame to be in a role would be between three to five years.
Achievements	Did you spend the last three years 'cruising' in your current role or did you contribute significantly to the company? How much has the business improved since you joined the company? What were your proudest achievements and are they relevant to the hiring company's current challenges?

Career history	To reduce the risk of hiring someone who might leave within a year, we study your track record to see if you have been a 'stayer' or 'quitter'. A string of one- to two-year stints in companies does not bode well. We also look for a pattern of growth in your previous years—were you given increasingly larger portfolios or sidelined for the past five years? Hiring managers also like to see if there is a clear pattern of career progression in these previous roles. The type of companies you have been with also matter as it reflects the environments you have been in and will be most comfortable with.

Six 'Keeps' to bear in mind

1. *Keep your Career Story visible in your CV.* Show that there has been a clear progression in your previous roles. You want the reader to be able to see that there is an upward trajectory to your career in terms of increasing geographical coverage, jobscope, product portfolio/revenue or even number of staff managed. This assures the hiring manager that you are growing and will continue to grow in their organisation.

2. *Keep it simple, keep it brief.* Include only relevant information and at the most, list down a maximum of four achievements for each role. Some candidates even list "Organiser for Dinner and Dance 2012" as their achievement, which leads us to conclude that it must have really been a highlight of an under-achieving career. Do not use tired clichés like 'possesses leadership and effective communication skills' or 'collaborated with partners and contributed to the bottom-line'. Leave such motherhood statements out of your CV as you are wasting valuable space for more relevant information.

3. *Keep it professional.* There is no need to include hobbies or leisure activities unless it is directly relevant to the role you are applying for. You need to pay attention to the smallest

details—even your contact email address. Including an email like sexmeup88@gmail.com or cyberthief-yolo@ hotmail.com does not exactly give the reader a great sense of confidence that you are serious about the role.

4. *Keep a list of keywords if it is a softcopy version.* If you are submitting a CV online or via email (which is usually the case these days), do include certain keywords in your document. If you are a supply planner with experience in Oliver Wight systems, please insert these two keywords into your text. This is because some recruiters will file away your resume into a central database and the next time a specific requirement like "Supply Planner with knowledge of Oliver Wight systems" comes up, the recruiter will do a search on 'Supply Planner' or 'Oliver Wight' and your profile will be flagged. Try to distill a dozen key words or skills and incorporate them into your CV. You would be surprised at how effective this guerrilla tactic could be.

5. *Keep it classy.* If you are sending a hardcopy resume, make sure you use good quality paper and ensure that the formatting, grammar and spelling is impeccable. Your CV is your career brochure and any signs of sloppiness or inferior quality will immediately reflect poorly on you. If you are submitting an electronic copy, the same rules apply. Ensure that you use a readable font like Times Roman (font size 10 to 12) or Arial (font size 10) and not more than two colours on your document. Have somebody with good English proofread your document to correct all errors.

6. *Keep it personal.* A nice touch to distinguish yourself from the fifty other applicants is to find out the HR or hiring manager for the role. Pick up the phone and call to find out who you should be addressing the document to. I am always pleasantly surprised to receive a resume addressed

to 'Mr Adrian Choo' rather than 'Dear Mr Recruiter' and tend to note the extra effort more favourably in my overall evaluation of the candidate.

Frequently Asked Questions on resume-writing

How long should my resume be?

As a general rule of thumb, if you are in your twenties, it should be no longer than two pages long. If you are in your thirties, no longer than three pages and for those in their forties, less than four pages. The ideal is still two pages and the maximum is four. Regardless of the age of the candidate, my ADHD-riddled brain will usually stop registering beyond the fourth page; and don't try to cheat by using font-size eight—tiny letters have a tendency to annoy.

How do I write my cover letter?

With as little ink as possible. As mentioned, your CV has only fifteen seconds of eye-time with the reader and you do not want this precious window to be wasted on deciphering a six-paragraph cover letter. The cover letter is meant to be a polite introduction of yourself, followed by a very brief summary of the three-biggest reasons of how your experience and expertise can help the company. Besides, most recruiters only glance briefly at the cover-letter before jumping straight into the resume, so don't sweat too much on it. Some even advise to not have a cover letter at all. I would not disagree.

Should I add a photograph to the CV?

This is a very common question and many HR practitioners are of two minds about it. To be honest, between two equally-qualified and suitable candidates, the better looking one will get the role. Research has shown that better looking candidates will stand a higher chance. So, will adding a photograph improve or diminish your chances of getting the first interview?

My advice is to err on the side of caution. Unless you have recently undergone extensive plastic surgery in Korea, you might want to leave your photograph out of your resume. Why subject yourself to the risk that the hiring manager thinks you remind him of his ex-wife or his childhood bully? There will be no marks deducted for not having a headshot of yourself, but it could work against you if you did, so why take the chance?

However, if you really want to include a photograph, please have it taken at a professional studio rather than using a selfie taken at last week's bachelorette party. It has to be in business attire and maybe even cleaned up using Photoshop (whether it is a little bit or a lot).

How far back into my career history should I go?

This largely depends on your age. Candidates in their early-fifties often find it difficult to place their entire career chronology into their resume. My advice would be to include at least the most recent (and relevant) second-half of their careers in the document, and then include a statement like "1978 to 1993—Various Sales/Marketing roles in US Companies—details available upon request." I know this makes you sound *really old*, but a fact is a fact and your age will come out sooner or later. For younger candidates, stopping at your first job will do. I have seen thirty-year-old candidates list "class monitor" (True story). Exclude anything that is not relevant.

Should I include my age or try to camouflage it?

It is illegal for employers to even ask for your age in some countries like the US and Australia. You do not have to state your age but you shouldn't try to camouflage it either. Experienced headhunters can generally guess your age using hidden cues like your year of graduation or the start-date of your first job. Some older candidates try to hide these by leaving such dates out. But omissions like these are automatic red-flags that the candidate is being cheeky. If the employer is a company that discriminates against older workers, overlooking the clear value and wisdom that they can bring to the table, then that is a company that you will not want to be a part of anyway.

Do I include my current and expected salary?

You should *never* include your salary in your resume as it is a highly confidential and personal piece of information. There is no guarantee that it won't fall into the wrong hands or is properly disposed of. Besides, an experienced recruiter would be able to accurately guess your salary package just by looking at your current company, job title and years of experience. I do not believe any star candidate has even been deprived of that first interview solely because his salary was not stated in his resume.

How much information should I put on LinkedIn?

LinkedIn is a valuable tool for increasing your exposure to the world. You should include the companies you have been with and the job titles while you were there. Inserting keywords would be helpful too. The important thing is not to include too many details, especially confidential company data you could be sued for. Some candidates innocently include information like "currently managing a US$23.6 million sales portfolio" or "on track to exceed 18.4 percent EBIT this coming year" which could make them unwitting accessories to an insider trading charge! Keep the information brief and leave your mobile or email contact so the recruiter can reach you for more details.

Why I didn't bother to read your resume

I receive countless unsolicited emails and CVs everyday. Over the years, I have devised my own 'algorithm' as to whether a CV gets responded to, filed or trashed.

I mean no disrespect to potential candidates, but it is simply impossible to respond to all mails arriving into my inbox. However, there are several types of emails/CVs that I will delete almost immediately without regret.

Emails that are not addressed to me personally

I get particularly annoyed by messages beginning with "Dear Recruiter" or "Dear Mr Boyden" (that's not even my name!). If you want me to invest my time to read your mail, the least you could do is to have the courtesy to find out who you are addressing your note to. If you are indeed spamming your CV to a hundred recipients, do it smartly with a mail-merge software that can insert my first name intelligently into the message.

Too many grammatical or spelling errors

My biggest turn-off is when I receive an email or CV with major spelling errors, or worse yet, basic grammatical errors. I am not talking about the usual 'neighbour vs neighbor' type typos, but the cringe-worthy "I have a good commanding of the English Linguage" types of errors. These mistakes are made even more glaring when the CV is transmitted in Microsoft word format, which highlights each transgression by underlining all errors in red and green. To me, it just shows that the candidate did not even bother enough to run a spellcheck or have someone proofread the document before sending it out.

Oversized emails

Yes, my internet connection at the office is a high-speed, 200GB per second one and my download speed is pretty decent. However, I do have a cap on my mailbox size and I do not appreciate the 7mb resume that you just emailed. Thinking that you just sent me both the old and new King James version of the Bible including illustrations, I open the file only to be greeted by a one page CV ... with a high-resolution 6.9mb passport-sized photograph of yourself. Whenever I receive files like these, the impression I get is that the candidate really isn't very tech-savvy or has a troubling phobia about asking others for help. In any event, I usually delete unsolicited CVs bigger than 1mb in size.

Groundhog Day CVs

Very often, I get CVs that look vaguely familiar. On closer inspection, I realise that the sender has emailed me that same unsolicited document at least four times over the past month. Even the introduction email is exactly the same, such that I think I'm in a *Star Trek* time-loop or experiencing Groundhog Day all over again. Please do not spam the headhunter.

Ghost emails

The final type of email that I almost always delete immediately is the one that has 'Job Wanted' in the subject line but absolutely no text in the body—and a word suspicious document named 'CV.doc' attached. Scarier still is when the sender's email is a cryptic-sounding ebola0032@gmail.com. Not knowing whether the sender is genuine or if the file contains more viruses than a sailor on shore leave, I always delete the entire email and block the sender forever.

Always remember that your resume is your 'professional brochure' and the sole objective of the CV is to earn you that coveted first interview. Make sure that everything is perfect and don't feel shy to ask your mentor for his/her advice.

Generally, try to make a personal connection with the recipient or even follow up with a phonecall a day later. This usually puts candidates in a more favourable light.

If you have a particularly challenging career history that makes resume-writing difficult, speak to an experienced career coach and invest in his/her time and advice—it will be well worth your time and money.

BONUS MATERIAL

What are the four phrases you should never use in your CV? Visit www.career-strategy.com/bonus and key in "phrases" to find out.

Chapter 9

Interview strategies

If you are an executive with at least ten to fifteen years of work experience, you have probably been conducting more interviews in your career than sitting in for them.

A job interview can be a scary event. Nobody likes to be picked apart and studied. However, if you are a senior executive, interviews should be approached more as a career discussion among equals, rather than an arms-folded 'so why do you want to work for me?' session, for as much as the prospective employer is selecting you, you are also selecting them—so this is a two-way street.

As a headhunter, I always walk my candidates, no matter how senior, through the interview process, coaching them on what to expect, how to answer and even what (not) to wear. However, not many readers will enjoy the benefits of a seasoned headhunter walking you through this ordeal, so this chapter hopes to prime you with the right attitude and hopefully, tools to navigate this important step in your career.

I prefer to call the interview 'career discussions' for senior-level positions, and treat them like a get-to-know-you session between the client and candidate. Like a first date, it is largely exploratory and both sides are trying to find out if there is a meeting of minds and a potential fit for both parties.

Interestingly, if you thought that interviews were stressful for the candidates, have you even considered where the burden of risk actually lies? If you don't get the job, life goes on as usual. However, for the hiring manager, a lot more hangs in the balance. What if he makes the wrong decision and offers the job to an incompetent liar who will make life miserable and ruin his reputation? Or what if he is facing the perfect candidate whom he cannot entice to join his team because of his poor interviewing or selling skills? From experience, the more critical the position is, the greater the degree of stress on the interviewer or employer, so as the interviewee, what is there to worry?

Is there a strategy to interviewing? Yes—and you need to get it right the first time because you usually only have one chance. The interview is a sales pitch with *you* as the product. You need to craft a message and send it across. What that message is and the manner you deliver it forms the basis of your strategy.

The first law of interviewing is to be over-prepared. Do your research on the company, the role, the competition and even on the interviewer. Know what they want and what you can do for them. I cannot over-emphasise this, but interview success is 90 percent preparation and 10 percent just being there. To land that dream job, you need to create an interview strategy that is effective and to-the-point.

The only three questions that matter

In the interview process, there are only three questions that matter to the interviewer. Everything else is peripheral and contingent on these three questions being answered satisfactorily.

Question 1: *Who is this guy?*

If a stranger on the street comes to you and says, "Hey Sir/ Madam, I can double your money in six months," wouldn't your first response be "Go away!"?

But if this person looks professionally dressed and says it with conviction, you will probably be intrigued and ask, "Who are you?"

Before explaining how you can be a huge asset to your future employer, you need to establish your credentials. If there is no credibility, nothing else you say will stick.

So if the stranger who promised to double your money replies that he's Donald Trump's private banker, you are definitely going to stop and listen. That is the power of establishing your credentials.

Similarly, you need to prepare a powerful response for the inevitable "Who are you?" question by telling your Career Story.

> YOUR CAREER STORY IS THE SET OF KNOWLEDGE,
> SKILLS, EXPERIENCE, ABILITIES, NETWORKS AND
> EXPERTISE THAT YOU HAVE ACQUIRED FROM EACH JOB
> IN YOUR CAREER HISTORY THAT MAKES YOU A BETTER-
> EQUIPPED PROFESSIONAL, ENABLING YOU TO PERFORM
> THE NEXT BIGGER ROLE THAT YOU ARE AIMING FOR.

We pick up skills, experience, knowledge and networks in every role and in every company we work for. Each will add value to our professional life in one way or another, be it at customer service, cross-cultural negotiation, or regional change-management.

To establish your credentials, you need to summarise your career history into a one-minute 'elevator pitch' highlighting your strengths and abilities. Your ability to distill the sets of experience and achievements at each company or role you have worked for and string them together as a coherent personal growth story will be crucial to cementing your credibility at the beginning of the career discussion. It provides a concise insight into where you've been and what you've done. Let's look at the following case study:

Andrew, HR Manager, CV

2008–present *Senior Regional HR Manager, Southeast Asia*
A multinational petrochemicals company

2004–2008 *Country HR Manager*
A US hedge fund covering mergers and acquisitions.

2001–2004 *Regional Compensation and Benefits Manager*
A US Bank

1998–2001 *Training Manager*
A US-based IT company

Andrew is now hoping to be selected for an HR Director, Asia-Pacific role with a US oil exploration company that is starting up in this region.

The hiring manager may think: This candidate's CV is all over the place. Like a rolling stone that gathers no moss, he has been hopping from one function to another, and switching industries from chemicals to IT and then to finance in a span of ten years. I can't figure this guy out. However, Andrew can frame his credentials correctly with a good Career Story:

I am a well-rounded HR Leader with in-depth experience in training, regional compensation and benefits, recruitment and talent development.

I am also skilled in general HR operations and have strong regional experience. Ten years of working in US MNCs has made me comfortable with the US corporate culture. In addition, in my role in setting up the HR operations for the new business unit makes me ideal for a start-up situation like yours. I am also IT and finance-savvy from my experience in the IT and the financial institution, and can assist in the ERP implementation you are currently undertaking, and also provide support with regards to the new company that you are in the process of acquiring. Moreover, I am in the same industry and have a thorough understanding of your market challenges and a proven track record of overcoming them.

See how Andrew's Career Story has unfolded, especially how each job experience now directly addresses the target company's own needs. He has shown how the knowledge and experience from each undertaking will enable him to complement and add value to the interviewer's company. By 'controlling the narrative' (a well-known PR strategy), Andrew was able to anchor himself as the perfect candidate in the interviewer's mind.

THE CAREER STORY SUMMARISES AND POSITIONS
YOUR SKILLSETS, FACILITATING THE HIRING MANAGER'S
THOUGHT-PROCESS IN HIS ASSESSMENT OF YOU. IT
PROVIDES A COHERENT CONTEXT AND FRAMEWORK

FROM WHICH YOU CAN STRUCTURE YOUR INDIVIDUAL
SELLING POINTS THAT MAKE YOU RELEVANT AND
ATTRACTIVE TO THE TARGET COMPANY.

So, the best answer to the question is to tell them your Career Story. It is the contextual thread that neatly ties up your past experiences in your previous companies.

So, what is *your* Career Story? Take the afternoon off, go somewhere quiet or retreat to your favourite Starbucks, then examine your resume, phase by phase. Create an inventory of your strengths, weaknesses, interests and passions, then juxtapose them alongside your list of skills learnt from each job. You will be surprised at how neatly everything falls into place.

Question 2: *What has he done before?*

This question is a double-barreled one—it is the hidden subtext that answers both the 'Who is this guy?' as well as the 'What can he do for me?' questions. The objective of this response should be to *establish your abilities*.

The biggest assurance that a candidate can and will perform in the future is his track record of similar successes in the past. During the career discussion, you will need to show what you have done in similar circumstances before and how you succeeded in those situations. You should be over-prepared for this question as it will strongly anchor the interviewer's opinions of you and influence his decision about you.

The best way of establishing your abilities is to tell them your success stories. Grab a pen and paper, then develop the success stories that highlight your particular skill or achievement. You need to prepare at least five success stories that you can talk about in detail. This is not just in preparation for the often-asked 'So what is your proudest achievement?' question but are bullet-points to bring up in the course of the interview to highlight your expertise or skills. By giving prepared, detailed examples, you display a great degree of confidence and honesty in answering questions and your credibility increases.

A candidate who pauses and is unable to recall details of the time he claimed to have doubled his company's sales will come across as unconvincing at best and dishonest at worst.

Always be honest and never make up your success stories. A skilled interviewer will always be able to spot a lie. My advice is to prepare at least five (or more) success stories, each pertaining to an achievement in your career that you are particularly proud of. Stories could include:

- *General Management.* How you penetrated a new market. How you increased EBIT by 25 percent. How you developed the regional strategy.
- *Sales Career.* How you built and managed the regional sales team. How you landed the biggest sales account in history. How you introduced a revolutionary new product or service.
- *HR Career.* How you implemented a new HR system. How you reduced employee turnover. How you conducted an employee engagement project.
- *Finance Career.* How you implemented a new ERP system. How you reorganised your regional finance team. How you saved the company millions by adding new controls.
- *Operations Career.* How you streamlined supply chain operations. How you increased the efficiency of your regional operations. How you rationalised the stock keeping units (SKUs) for the local market.

Now that you have your list of proudest career achievements in mind, is there a way to structure each success story effectively?

I recommend using a 'Six-step Answer' to answer this question. It follows a fixed format and with sufficient practice, each story will roll off your tongue naturally and you would have a very convincing list of achievements to talk about.

Six-step Answer
1. State the achievement (usually to resolution of a major or challenging problem).
2. What did you do to identify the root of the problem?
3. What was the solution? (prepare to explain your rationale)
4. What was the biggest challenge you faced? How did you overcome it? (usually resistance from people)
5. What was the outcome? (be specific)
6. What did you learn from all this?

Example 1
(#1) My Proudest Achievement was when I identified a new market segment that no one was servicing. (#2) I studied it and discovered that it was potentially worth $65 million a year and found that my company had the capability to tap into this segment. (#3) I convinced the senior management and engineering teams to design a new service package especially for the market and launched the product myself. (#4) The biggest challenge was selling the idea to the Board of Directors but I backed up my business case with solid numbers, projections and product mock-ups. (#5) In the end, our product captured 86 percent of that market, creating an entirely new revenue stream for the company. This concept has been adopted on a global basis and now represents 12 percent of the total revenues. (#6) I learnt that one needs to be highly entrepreneurial to thrive in our market.

Example 2
(#1) My proudest achievement was to outsource the warehousing and supply chain function to a third party logistic company. (#2) I noticed that our high rental and manpower costs did not justify the turnover of products from our warehouse. And from my calculations, we could save up to S$4 million a year. (#3) I conducted a study to verify this, then identified and evaluated three companies who could do this for us. After awarding the tender, I rewrote the entire "Service Level Agreements" to ensure there were no problems. (#4) The biggest challenge was selecting the right

partner to work with and I conducted extensive research and discussions to find the best one. (#5) As a result, we saved more than $5 million a year and improved customer satisfaction by over 44 percent! (#6) My biggest learning lesson was to base business decisions on hard facts and numbers, not on emotions.

Applying the 'Six-step Answer' to any career success story gives you a structured approach to sharing the achievement more effectively. As always, you need to practise. Make the story-telling smooth and natural and master it like the back of your hand.

Question 3: *What can he do for me?*

Remember that the interview is a sales pitch and the product is you. Let's say you are purchasing a new vacuum cleaner. After you are comfortable with the brand and reputation of the product, you will probably wonder, "What can this do for me?"

So what if the vacuum cleaner is the most energy efficient in the market or comes in the hottest shade of Ferrari red? If these attributes are not important to you, does it matter at all? However, if you are a family man with young children, you might be more interested in the fact that the filter is Hepa-3 rated and is able to remove bacteria or that it is ultra-silent, so you can clean the house while the children are asleep.

We are only interested in attributes that benefit us directly, so if the salesperson knows these hot-buttons, the sale is going to be easier to make. Likewise, to sell yourself more effectively, you need to find out more information before the interview:

- What is the CEO's strategy for the region? Aggressive or sustainable growth? Organic growth via acquisitions?
- What are the organisation's three biggest challenges? What are the bottlenecks or pain-points?
- Is this a newly created role? What happened to the incumbent?
- What attributes/skillsets are needed for success in this role?

Once you are able to identify the relevant information, you will be able to craft *both* your Career Story and your success stories to cater *specifically* to the organisation's needs.

For example, if the target company is facing trouble implementing their new multi-million dollar Enterprise Resource Planning (ERP) system, prepare a success story on how you have seamlessly implemented a similar one for your current company. Or if the company is having a tough time launching a new product in China—demonstrate your expertise by sharing a success story on how you have successfully introduced a similar product in that market.

By understanding what the target company requires, you are able to tailor your pitch to suit their specific needs, making you more valuable to them compared to other less-prepared candidates. You will also be able to better understand their challenges and have a more meaningful engagement to make an informed decision about whether the role is something you would be comfortable in and excel at.

But how would you find out about these needs? There are several sources. You are probably in the same industry as the target company, so having your ears to the ground and finding out what those challenges are should be quite straightforward.

If you are being managed by a headhunter for the role, milk him for all the information. If he is a good one, he should have shared all this with you, otherwise, press him to find out more.

Another way you can get such inside information is by asking friends who are working in the target company. You need to be careful to (a) protect the source of the information, and (b) not ask sensitive questions that could be misconstrued as industrial espionage, so be careful gathering intelligence using this method.

Some market information is easily available over the internet. Run a detailed Google search and you would be surprised how much data regarding their recent M&A, downsizing, or even market-entry plans are available online. Some of these data can be found in investor briefings, company annual reports and speeches made by the CEO. Often, the most salient information can be gleaned by re-reading the job description alone. If it states 'Strong Knowledge of Implementing Regional Supply Chain Solutions required' then it is probably a hint that the company needs to hire someone who is an expert at this.

In summary, by knowing exactly what the target company wants and crafting your Career Story and success stories to specifically address these needs, you are positioning yourself in the most attractive way to them during the career discussion.

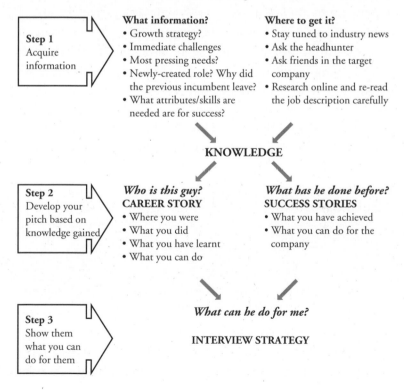

Step 1
Acquire information

What information?
• Growth strategy?
• Immediate challenges
• Most pressing needs?
• Newly-created role? Why did the previous incumbent leave?
• What attributes/skills are needed are for success?

Where to get it?
• Stay tuned to industry news
• Ask the headhunter
• Ask friends in the target company
• Research online and re-read the job description carefully

KNOWLEDGE

Step 2
Develop your pitch based on knowledge gained

Who is this guy?
CAREER STORY
• Where you were
• What you did
• What you have learnt
• What you can do

What has he done before?
SUCCESS STORIES
• What you have achieved
• What you can do for the company

Step 3
Show them what you can do for them

What can he do for me?

INTERVIEW STRATEGY

Frequently Asked Questions on interviews

Why do interviewers sometimes ask silly questions?

"How do you know if a tree is stable?" (Google)
"How many lamp-posts are there from their airport to our office?" (BP)
"What would you do if you became the Minister for Tourism?" (Shell)

These are actual interview questions used by hiring managers. The main purpose is often to judge how you would respond to curveball situation and how you would react when put in a spot.

However, these silly questions are often used to examine your thought processes and how you think. For instance, responding to the last question with something frivolous like "I would increase tourist numbers by putting up big banners at our airport to welcome visitors!" will not highlight your intellect in a flattering manner. (Why would you put banners *inside* the airport? Haven't the visitors *already* arrived?) I would answer:

As the Minister of Tourism, the key objective of my job would be to increase visitor numbers and tourist-dollar spend, hence I would first conduct studies to uncover which countries have the highest numbers of visitors, and more importantly, which ones spend the most and why. Because marketing resources are limited, I would focus on the top three countries with the most 'spending tourists' and drive campaigns at them. I would even get local hotels to co-sponsor these ads so we can have an even wider reach with our limited budget.

Having answered in this fashion, you would have exhibited a big-picture view with a carefully thought-out strategy and understanding of how to leverage your resources through partnership. There is never a right or wrong answer to these types of questions. The interviewer just wants to observe your thought process.

If there are three interviewers, who do I make the most eye contact with?

Spend about half of your eye contact time looking at the one who is asking you the question, dividing the balance between the other two. Do not ignore anyone for you would never know if the quiet and unassuming lady in the corner is the secretary or the global head of HR. If there are more than three interviewers, make a conscious effort to look in the direction of all of them as you are talking, trying hard not to make anyone feel left out.

What should I not do during an interview?

You should never speak badly of your ex-boss or former company, no matter how miserably you were treated in the past. This is a very serious faux-pas which basically tells your potential boss that he will probably get slimed by you when you leave his employment. Keep it professional.

Is there any term that I should not use?

Of all the taboo phrases to avoid during a career discussion, the worst would be 'work-life balance'. Used in a sentence, "I value work-life balance" or "Does this job offer work-life balance?" or "What is the company's stance towards work-life balance?" will never come across in any positive way.

Sure, by 'work-life balance', you mean not slaving away for the company every evening of the week and burning all my weekends with unnecessary meetings. However, to the interviewer, all he is hearing is, "I've decided to take it easy and want to go home at 5.30pm every day." Should this phrase be mentioned by a female candidate, then fairly or unfairly, images of her carrying crying babies will start floating into mind. Interviews have tanked simply on this phrase alone. There is no upside to mentioning this, so strike it out of your interview vocabulary.

What is the biggest mistake to make in an interview?

Going in unprepared. No, you do not want to try winging the interview. If you really want the job, do your homework on the company and their products. I have seen candidates talk at length about a product range that was discontinued a year ago. It was like watching a car crash in slow motion. Like a first date, you want to appear knowledgeable to the interviewer so you can leave a positive impression. I would even go the extra mile to find out who the interviewer would be and a quick LinkedIn or Google search before meeting him.

What questions do I ask the interviewer?

In legal-themed television serials, the older and more experienced lawyer will always tell his junior, "When in front of the judge/jury, never ask the witness a question you don't already know the answer to." Similarly, the 'so, do you have any questions to ask me?' part of the interview can actually be gamed to your advantage to slip in any additional points about your profile/ability that may not have been covered earlier in the discussion.

For instance, you could ask, "What are the most important attributes needed to succeed in this role?" The hiring manager will rattle off a list of abilities/skills, and after he is done, you respond with, "Yes, Attributes A, B and C are indeed critical for this role, that's why I'm quite comfortable with it as I have <insert your achievements highlighting Attribute A, B & C here>."

Another good question is "What is the career progression path for this position?" which indicates you are a 'stayer' and want to contribute to the organisation beyond the role, which significantly increases your brownie points.

Other than talking, what is the other most important thing at an interview?

Observe everything. Observe how your future boss conducts himself and whether you would like working for him. Observe whether he is checking his phone every two minutes for mail or whether he respectfully puts it away for the duration of the interview. Observe whether the office has more empty seats than there are workers as it could be a sign they are downsizing. Feel the energy and buzz in the office (or lack thereof) to get an idea of the working culture there. As you walked through the door, were you greeted warmly or did a disgruntled staff just wave you in, muttering that opening the door wasn't in her job description. Keep your eyes open and pick up as many clues as you can.

Do you have tips about interviewing through skype or video conference?

Videoconferencing used to be the main preserve of high-end companies who could afford the exorbitant ISDN charges but in today's connected world, it is being increasingly replaced by Skype, the free PC-based solution. However, many of us are still not fully comfortable talking into a box, so the following tips will help you through this:

- *Speak slowly.* Many times, the person at the other end of the line may not be of the same nationality or culture as you, and may not comprehend you at your normal talking speed. Moreover, the internet connection may not be a stable one and the transmission may not be perfect. Slow down and enunciate each word carefully to avoid misunderstandings.
- *Make sure there are no background noises.* Make sure you are in a quiet place with a strong wifi signal. You do not want to be distracted during the skype call or suffer intermittent connection that could throw you off your game.

- Sometimes, you are scheduled to speak with someone in a different time-zone. It could even be at 6am your local time. *Do wake up at least a half hour before to fully come to your senses.* You don't want to appear to be in a daze.
- *If you are taking the skype call at home, remember to wear pants.* I know the camera captures images from the chest upwards, but one candidate knocked over his desktop camera to the floor and ... let's just say, it was hilarious (though not for him, I'm sure).

BONUS MATERIAL

Visit www.career-strategy.com/bonus and key in "likeme" to learn about the three best ways to get the interviewer to like you.

Chapter 10

Salary strategies

There is a scene from the movie *Pretty Woman* starring Julia Roberts and Richard Gere which I always refer to when I coach my team on negotiation.

It is the bathtub scene where Gere's character, the ultra-rich corporate raider Edward Lewis wanted to hire Robert's character, a prostitute named Vivian Ward, for a week. The conversation went like this: "I would like you to spend the week with me, I would like to hire you as an employee. I would pay you to be at my beck and call. I want a professional."

Excited at the prospect of having a fulltime job for a week, Vivian said, "If you're talking twenty-four hours a day, it's gonna cost you."

"Give me a ball-park figure. How much?"

"Four thousand."

He immediately responded with, "Two thousand."

"Three thousand."

"Done!" The corporate raider declared.

A few scenes later, Vivian confessed, "You know, I would have stayed for two thousand dollars…"

"And I would have gladly paid four." He smiled.

Someone once said that a deal is defined as an agreement reached where both sides feel they have outwitted the other. Salary negotiations can feel that way. Some companies think they can get the most out of their employees by paying low wages and extracting long hours.

These discussions are often uncomfortable situations and could even be taboo to some. This is especially so in an Asian environment where it is regarded rude to talk about how much money you earn, let alone asking for. As such, one question I am always asked is, "How do I talk about the money?"

Before delving into the strategies for salary negotiation, let's start with basic principles of a salary.

What is a salary?

In ancient Rome, soldiers were paid in silver and salt (*'salarius'* in Latin). This was because this life-saving crystal was in such short supply, it was considered to be very valuable (which is where the term "he is not worth his salt" originates from).

We are so used to receiving our monthly pay and often don't think much about it. It goes into our bank account and disappears into the ether of unknown expenditure.

But if we consider it as the payment for services rendered to your company, then it might change your perspective a little.

Like the $10 you paid to the kid to mow your lawn, or the horticulturist you paid $500 to ensure your daffodils thrive in optimal soil conditions, their salary is what you exchange in return for a benefit that they provide you.

Likewise, your salary is paid to you for the value that you bring to the company—it is important to adopt this frame of mind when discussing salaries with your prospective employer because understanding how you can add value to their business strengthens your bargaining power.

Components of your annual remuneration

When talking about salaries, we often refer to the amount we receive at the end of the month. Sometimes, we talk about the year-end bonus as well. However, to have a meaningful discussion, we need to understand what our annual remuneration comprises—typically of the guaranteed and non-guaranteed components, incentives and expatriate benefits. Together, these parts make up your On-Target Earnings (OTE).

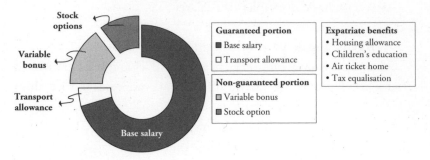

Components of your annual remuneration

Guaranteed portion	Expatriate benefits
■ Base salary	• Housing allowance
☐ Transport allowance	• Children's education
	• Air ticket home
Non-guaranteed portion	• Tax equalisation
▨ Variable bonus	
■ Stock option	

Guaranteed component

This largely comprises the monthly amount that is paid to you. Often called the base salary or monthly salary, some companies pay it in twelve calendar months while others may pay you in thirteen. Either way, this part is guaranteed no matter how terribly the company (or you) performs.

The other part that is guaranteed is usually the transport allowance, especially if your job requires car travel. If you are senior enough, some companies may choose to provide you with a vehicle instead of this monthly stipend. Most times, when candidates negotiate salary, they seem more focused on this part of the equation, which may not be the best strategy.

Non-guaranteed component

This part of the total remuneration package is where things get interesting. For most companies, this takes the form of variable bonuses or if your job is a sales-related one, commissions.

Most companies structure their compensation plan on a 80/20 split. That is, the guaranteed part forms 80 percent of the total package, with an upside of another 20 percent upon achieving targets. For example, if your total OTE is $250,000 a year, your base salary will be $200,000 (80 percent) and your bonuses will be S$50,000 (20 percent). Some companies want to stress on performance and may offer more aggressive splits between guaranteed and non-guaranteed components; like 70/30 or 60/40. Some sales roles have gone as far as a 50/50 split. However, these ratios are meaningless unless we study the numbers closely. For example, which would you rather have?

Example:	Projected OTE:
a) 50/50 OTE split at base salary of $160,000/yr	$320,000/year
OR	
b) 80/20 OTE split at base salary of $200,000/yr	$250,000/year
OR	
c) 60/40 OTE split at base salary of $180,000/yr	$300,000/year

Option (a) looks like the best choice at first, given that the total projected OTE is $320,000 per year, it offers the highest pay-out on the board. However, this works on the *assumption* that you will be able to achieve all targets that have been set before you. If you miss your targets entirely, you will walk away with $160,000 in basic salary only.

You may also have noticed that option (b) has the highest base salary of $200,000 a year and riding on this alone makes it the most attractive arrangement regardless of company or personal performance. However, the upside potential is limited to another $50,000 which makes it the least exciting outcome in terms of annual remuneration.

Option (c) might provide a safer middle ground between the other two options, resting at a higher base salary but also having better potential rewards.

Incentives

Companies will try their best to retain their top talent and one effective method is to give them financial incentives over and above their basic salary—often in the form of stock options, restricted stock or cash in the form of retention bonuses. These incentives are sometimes jokingly referred to as 'Golden Handcuffs', which makes it painful for staff to give up and leave for another company.

While these sweeten the deal, remember that they are not guaranteed. For example, the exercise price could be below your purchase price or if the start-up you joined never got listed.

Expatriate packages

If you are being relocated to work in another country, you should expect to be provided an expatriation package, which would include housing, transport, children's education, cost-of-living allowances (or COLA) and even annual air tickets home for the family.

While this may allow you to live like a king in some third world nation, remember that this component forms part of your total remuneration and could be taxable in some countries. So, whatever you receive, ask for tax equalisation, which essentially puts you in an 'equalised state' of tax as if you were based in your original country of residence so that you are tax neutral.

The various components of your annual remuneration are necessary to define and examine each component when negotiating your salary. You need to look at the *entire package* and instead of individual parts or you will lose sight of the big picture. It also allows you to choose the salary strategy that matches your situation at the new company.

For instance, if you feel that the new company has products or services that may not work out in the first few years, you might want to choose a 80/20 OTE split just to hedge your bets. Alternatively, if you are confident of delivering results at your new company, then you may want to opt for the 50/50 OTE split with a high base (you're such an expert now, you can even understand the jargon). If you have absolute confidence in yourself, you might even be bold enough to suggest a ridiculously low base plus everything on commission with an unlimited upside arrangement.

REAL-LIFE CAREER STORY

David Choe, Artist

David Choe is a renowned American-Korean graffiti artist based in Los Angeles. He has always been in great demand for painting murals and was asked by Sean Parker (a famous internet entrepreneur) to paint a mural at a small internet start-up in Silicon Valley in 2005.

He was offered US$60,000 in cash or in equivalent amount in stock. At that time, he thought that the company's products were ridiculous and pointless but being the anti-establishment artist he was, he chose the stock anyway.

Seven years later, the company went public and his stock options were worth US$200 million overnight. He never imagined that such a ridiculous and pointless company like Facebook could ever list at $38 per share.

What determines your remuneration?

Before you even begin salary negotiations, you need to recognise the contributing factors that determine your offer package. This empowers you to negotiate on each factor to build a compelling case as to why you should command a premium over the next candidate. These factors are summarised as such:

What determines your remuneration

- *Demand for your skill/network/knowledge.* Your value to the company is usually the sum total of the skill/network/knowledge/expertise that you can bring to them. If the skills you have are rare and your market knowledge deep compared to others in the talent pool, your bargaining power increases.
- *Your track record.* Having a particularly valuable skill won't matter if you do not have a recent track record of success in the area. You may have been a top surgeon but if your last five patients died on the operating table, you will have a tough time convincing others that you are good at what you do.
- *Your years of experience.* Malcolm Gladwell in *Outliers* estimates that it takes around 10,000 hours to fully master a skill. So the more experience you have at the job or in the industry, the more peace of mind the employer has that you can perform. Have you hit your 10,000-hour mark yet?
- *Your qualifications.* For certain technical roles or specialised industries, having specific certification can add a premium to your candidature. Sometimes, having a 'branded' degree from Harvard or MIT further enhances your positioning.

- *Amount of work/scope the job requires.* Is the role a local, regional or global one? Salary bands increase with similar increases in scope and if the job is going to keep you up all night with conference calls to third-world countries, there must be a premium. Besides geographic scope, other considerations include whether this is an individual contributor or a team leadership role, or a single or multiple portfolio one. The salary often commensurates with the revenue size of the business too—a person handling a $50 million one will not command as high a package as someone in charge of a $500 million one.
- *Your employer's budget.* No matter how qualified you are for the role, the final package is often dictated by the company's budget. A technology client of mine has a policy of paying top dollar for top performers, believing that you get what you pay for and are often flexible for the right candidates. Over the years, I have seen the fruits of such a strategy and am glad to say that it works. Conversely, some companies will stick rigidly to the budget set up by HR—no amount of negotiation can alter what has already been cast in stone, no matter how much value or increased sales the candidate can bring to the company.

Three caveats when discussing salary

Now that you are familiar with the 'levers' that affect the final package, you will be better prepared for the salary negotiation.

Caveat #1: Money is emotional

Money doesn't just represent the purchasing power it brings but is often associated with a person's ego and social stature. Getting a hefty increase really strokes the ego. It sends the message that the company values your potential contribution and makes you feel like it justifies the feeling you've been having all this time—that your current company never really appreciated your hard work and effort. However, getting a pay cut may feel like you have just been shortchanged, no matter what the other positive factors of the job may be. Whatever the case, money is always emotional—that is why whenever candidates say 'It's not about the money', I always take it with a pinch of salt.

This means that during the salary negotiation, do not let your feelings get the better of you. Look at the big picture and think rationally. You may feel entitled to that 30 percent increase in salary, but can the start-up company you are joining really afford to pay you that? Take a step back and not see the forest for the trees.

REAL-LIFE CAREER STORY

Antoine, Regional Director

Antoine was a candidate I found while conducting a search for a fast-growing medical devices company. The role was for a Managing Director for a rather large business unit overseeing a $250 million portfolio.

When I approached him in 2009, he had just been retrenched by his company as it was 'rightsizing'. As their regional director (he was an expatriate), his salary was the biggest cost on the spreadsheet and HQ decided he was no longer needed. He had been out of work for almost seven months and confessed he was going to run out of money soon.

This role was ideal for him and he was excited. However, the position did not come with any expatriate benefits (no housing, car or children's education). His previous salary was US$600,000 a year, including all the perks, but the salary my client was offering was (in his own words) "merely US$550,000 a year" on a strictly local term.

Bearing in mind that this was during the financial crisis, where juicy roles like these were few and far between, he actually turned down the offer. His reason was, "I refuse to take a pay cut especially when there are no expat benefits. It would be would be embarrassing if my peers found out. I shall wait for a better offer."

A year after that incident, I met a mutual friend and was told that he was unemployed for a total of fourteen months, borrowing money from banks and friends before he finally decided to pack up and head home, leaving behind a mountain of debt and unpaid bills.

Caveat #2: Salary should not be the sole (or even the main) consideration

It is often a difficult thing to do, but you need to ask yourself: Salary aside, is this role congruent with my Career Strategy?

You might want to pivot into an industry you do not have much experience in, but wish to get a foothold in. You might get an offer from an exciting start-up company you have always wanted to work for but the role is one level below where you are at right now. Or you may feel that you are financially stable at your phase in life and would like to focus more on non-monetary aspects like career-fulfillment or just more time with your family.

These are times when looking at the bigger picture helps—and you will realise that money might just be a 'hygiene factor' after all (a nice-to-have but not key motivational factor, as attributed to Frederick Herzberg motivation-hygiene theory).

REAL-LIFE CAREER STORY

Adrian Choo, Headhunter

Straight after my stint at GE Plastics, I was a high-energy 32-year-old who was at my first career crossroad. I realised that after seven years of working, I had the soft skills for sales, business development, people-management and leadership but no industry-specific knowledge to carve a vertical niche. I wanted to find a new career where I could pivot all my strengths and passion for career counselling into a new job.

That was when I decided to get into executive search. I knew I had to start at the top with a top tier global company, but the world of retained executive search was a very exclusive one and difficult to penetrate.

I interviewed at Boyden and began my career there as a consultant, the second-lowest rung on the headhunting food chain. I also took a tremendous pay-cut off my base salary, which was painful. However, I knew I had to learn the ropes and consoled myself that it was my tuition fees to get into the industry. A part of my ego told me not to do it but I felt it was a necessary step to re-tool myself for the next phase of my career.

After two solid years of acquiring new skills and learning the business, I was performing so well that I started earning more than I did at my old job in GE. I have never looked back to that point in my career when I took a bet on myself and won. I realised that while the salary was important, we should never lose sight of our Career Strategy.

Caveat #3: Keep it professional

I have seen salary negotiations go badly—mostly horror-stories from friends in HR. Because money can make people emotional, some candidates have gotten upset when their expectations were not met. They pouted, got frustrated and sometime even lost their cool. Other sales-focused executives automatically go into 'horse-trading' mode and start pushing—"How about another $500 more a month? No? How about $350? No? How about throwing in petrol allowance? The other company that's courting me is giving me $200 in dental benefits—can you match?"

Horse-trading leaves a bad aftertaste and makes you look petty, so please refrain from doing it. Always keep a calm and professional demeanour when discussing salaries, or better still, let the headhunter handling your case do it for you.

BONUS MATERIAL

Should you trust your headhunter to negotiate your salary for you or should you insist on doing it yourself? Login to www.career-strategy.com/bonus and key "DIY" to access this extra article.

General strategies for salary negotiation

There is a strategy for everything. Bear in mind the following general strategies and your chances of a successful salary negotiation will improve significantly.

Try to get as much an uplift as possible

The goal is to get as much of a salary increase as possible. After all, every job change is fraught with uncertainty and this risk factor should be mitigated with a premium. The big question is knowing *how much* to ask. Do your research—ask the headhunter, your friends in the industry or even the hiring manager.

Negotiate individual components

Knowledge is power, and thanks to your smart career move of purchasing and reading this book, you now know what components to negotiate. Try to move each individual portion upwards—ask for a healthy base salary to begin with, then try to get more upside through the variable bonuses. Next, try to nudge their incentive scheme upwards. Of course, you need to know what is negotiable and what isn't so you don't behave too much like a thug by this point. For instance, some companies have salary bands and if you are at the top of that range, they may not be able to raise it (one professional tip is to ask to be upgraded to the next band), or the variable bonus may be limited to three months and cannot be altered, then no amount of table banging could change that.

Be bold

I am a staunch believer of the 'don't ask, won't know' school of thought. Be bold (but not unreasonable) when asked for an expected salary. Push your luck a little but don't be too pushy.

Know your own value

Know where you stand in the market. Are you clearly the only person in the industry who has the track record to resolve the company's specific challenge (eg. Increasing sales of MRI machines to hospitals in the region)? If you are, then you have strong bargaining power.

Excel during the interview

If you blow the interviewers away with your stellar performance during the interviews, they will be bending over backwards to have you on the team. Conversely, if you performed badly, you will have an uphill battle justifying that premium.

Don't forget the Stress/Dollar Factor the new job brings

Remember the concept discussed in "Should you stay or leave?" in Chapter 5? Always be mindful that with every extra dollar that is given, an extra dollar (or four) is expected from you in terms of commitment and deliverables. One candidate was interviewing for a role with a strategy consulting firm where the expected salary was about $250,000 a year, but he was expected to bring in four-times that amount in new business. He was so bold as to ask for double that and my client responded with, "Sure! I'll even give you a million if you can commit to bringing in $4 million. You might not even have the time to spend your money then— are you game for that?" You really need to know what you are getting yourself into.

Know when to walk away

As Kenny Roger's famous song goes, "You need to know when to hold 'em, know when to fold 'em, know when to walk away, know when to run." Likewise, know the range of remuneration for which you will be happy with or to fold your cards and go home.

Frequently Asked Questions on salary negotiation

How much of an increment should I ask for when switching jobs?

This is a trick question. You should ask for as much as possible ... but *how much* should you expect to get? That's another question.

The quick answer is that it depends on your:

- *Current Salary.* If you have been at your company for many years and the annual increments have been around three to four percent, you might feel that your salary has been unfairly depressed compared to market rates. Worse still, if your company has a reputation for paying below market rates, then your current salary level is probably below par. If the company you are joining has a decent salary policy, you should ask for a market-rate salary or at least, a 20 to 25 percent uplift (or even 30 percent). However, if you feel you are already at market rates, then a 10 to 20 percent uplift would not be unreasonable in today's economy.

- *Current age.* From our twenties to late-thirties when the base salary is lower, a 15 to 20 percent increase is reasonable. However, for a senior executive in his forties to fifties, a 20 percent increase in salary of say, S$400,000 a year would translate to a hefty S$80,000 jump which may be tough for some employers to swallow. Typically, there is a salary arc where the older you get, or more highly you're paid, the less your salary improvement. However, if you have managed to keep your skills and Career Strategy fresh and on track, you could keep your increases in the 15 to 20 percent band. Otherwise, a 10 to 15 percent increase would be fair to expect.

- *Current format.* Sometimes, the trick is not in getting an absolute dollar increase but in the format. If the new company doesn't have the budget for what you are asking for, you could ask them to top up the figure through a special performance bonus tied to KPIs. One candidate asked for a $300,000 package but the client could only give $270,000. I advised my client to give him the remaining $30,000 in achievement bonuses at year end, or even upfront as a sign-on bonus.

- *Skills and marketability.* Of course, if you have a rare skill or knowledge that employers need, then the bargaining power is with you. Make this clear and play it to your advantage.

In summary, when changing jobs, you should generally expect around 10 to 20 percent above your current salary, however, there are a lot of variables that come into play. Do not just look at the money side of the equation but also what you have to give up for the salary increase (family time, a stress-free life, etc)— does the increase in salary commensurate with the increase in travel, responsibilities, and midnight conference calls? Be wise.

How do I answer questions about my expected salary?

It is best to ask them what range they have in mind, or if they really push for it, be transparent and give a number that you would be truly happy with. Better still, if you have a headhunter to represent you, let him do the talking. If he is a seasoned one, he will be able to get a good deal for you. After all, he bills the client a percentage of your package, hence it is in his interest that you get as good a deal possible.

Where can I get salary data to benchmark myself?

Go online—there are a number of sites that have such data freely available. But take it as a rough gauge for it only provides an estimated figure. Moreover, your industry may not be listed in that database.

The salary negotiation phase of the process need not be a nasty or stressful one. Just be genuine, reasonable and understand where the prospective employer is coming from. Keep in mind your Career Strategy and incorporate the lessons in this chapter into your game plan.

Chapter 11

Accepting the offer

So, they have finally made you an offer and all you need to do to seal the deal is to sign the offer letter. But before you sign on the dotted line, take a step back, and ask yourself some questions.

Will this opportunity improve my life?

Will this new job make you happier or more satisfied with your career? Is it going to positively affect your self-confidence, health and family life? If the new role is going to bring more work stress and/or disharmony to your relationships, you need to think really hard about moving forward.

Have I checked with my spouse?

A change in job is a major decision and will affect the entire family. Have you spoken to your spouse/partner about it? Is he/she supportive of the move? The new role may require longer hours and more travel—has the childcare logistics been settled?

Does this move fit into my Career Strategy?

Is the job in line with your future goals two jobs down the road and does it leverage on your strengths, passion and skills? Is the industry you are getting into a growth or sunset one? Is there better career progression at the new company as compared to the current one? How will this role improve and enhance your ongoing Career Story?

Will I enjoy this role or am I doing this just for the money?

Is this new job going to be more fun than your current one, or will it be even more stressful and frustrating? What are your *real* reasons for accepting this offer—is it only for the better salary?

Have I done my due diligence on the company and/or boss?
Are you familiar with the company's future strategy or product line-up? Are these financially stable? Is this a hire-and-fire company or one with a heart? Have they been re-organising their business units repeatedly in the last few years? (A very big red flag.) Is their CEO doing a great job or has he recently been replaced? Have you met your new boss and had time to size him up—do you know what his work ethic or reputation in the industry is like? Is he an easy boss or a notorious micro-manager? You need to have a good understanding of your new environment to minimise any sudden and rude shocks after joining the new team.

Will I be a good cultural fit?
Different companies have different cultures and it can be challenging to adapt to the new one if the changes are too drastic. One senior candidate spent two decades in progressive US MNCs before he suddenly decided to join a Japanese competitor. The absolute lack of decision-making authority and consensus-seeking culture was too much for him to bear and he quit after three short and painful months.

Have I met my team?
A lot of your success depends on your colleagues and direct reports. Having weak and dysfunctional, or worst still, hostile, team mates could quickly sink your hopes for a successful transition. There have been many horror stories of candidates who turn up on the first day of work only to find a team of resentful folks who were unhappy that the job went to an outsider and wanted to prove that the appointment was a mistake. Meeting the team and understanding their strengths and weaknesses will enable you to make a better decision as to whether you want to invest the next years of your life with the new company or not.

Am I clear on my KPIs, goals, scope, geography and degree of travel?

Even though things may change after you sign up, it is important to have clarity on how you will be assessed, the extent of your regional coverage and the teams you are working with or have been put in charge of. This will reduce future confusion should the scope change.

Am I comfortable with the salary and bonus scheme?

Have the terms of compensation been made clear or are there parts of the contract you are still unsure of? Such as a vaguely worded clause on how the Employee Stock Options plan will be structured? Are you certain of the details and breakdown of perks (eg. business class travel for flights lasting more than five hours), transport allowances, etc? Are you comfortable with the KPIs upon which your annual performance bonus will be calculated? These important details need to be sorted out either with the headhunter or with HR before you sign with the company.

Is there an unfair non-competition clause and does this company have a reputation for enforcing it?

Restrictive covenants are almost standard in most employment contracts today. These clauses state that if you leave the company, you are not allowed to work for a competitor for a certain period of time or you could be sued.

While it may be worrying to agree to a non-competition clause, many of these clauses are deemed as 'against public policy' by the Courts unless they are reasonably worded. Often, these safeguards are put in by the company to protect their trade secrets or confidential information. However, it is largely up to the Employer to specify exactly what they are protecting.

Have that clause removed if you are uncomfortable with it. However, if you are unable to do so, try to find out if the company has been overzealous in enforcing these non-competition clauses through the courts. If they are, then you minimise your risk by not agreeing to it. If you are in need of more information, engage a lawyer who is familiar with such 'Restraint of Trade' actions.

As mentioned, a job change is a major life event. Before accepting the offer, be aware of the issues that could complicate things for you. Join the new company with your eyes wide open to minimise the attendant risks involved.

BONUS MATERIAL

My employer is suing me for a breach of non-competition clause. What should I do? Visit www.career-strategy.com/bonus and key in "lawsuit" to find out more.

Chapter 12

Resigning with grace
and dignity

So, you've decided to join the new company and have signed the offer letter. Some thoughts will now run through your mind: What do I do next? How do I inform my boss and how will he react? What if he makes a counter-offer?"

These are all valid questions at this offer and acceptance stage. The anxiety is heightened for those who have not switched jobs much in their career or have been in their company for a long time. Consider these tips before signing on the dotted line.

Make up your mind before you sign the letter of offer

Many candidates get infatuated with the attention the prospective employers have been lavishing on them, or get so distracted by the hefty increase in salary, that they get carried away and accept the letter of offer without fully understanding the ramifications of their actions. These candidates sign the letter of offer and then get cold feet when their spouse gets upset at 'the dumbest idea of their life' or their boss begs or threatens them when they break the news or the organisation makes a counter-offer that is too good to refuse. They then have to renege on the new offer and disappoint everyone in the process.

Think about all aspects of this move clearly before accepting the offer. Re-read the previous chapter if you need to. Have you spoken to your spouse about it? Do you have his/her buy-in? One candidate's husband refused to let her sign the offer letter because she would be earning more money than him. Having the blessings of your partner (or at the very least, not being vetoed) is very important because it would be difficult to make such a major move without the support. More importantly, you need to understand that family life often as important as work life and you should never jeopardise it with rash or unilateral decisions.

Have you thought long and hard about the new role, the organisation and the opportunities? How about the new commitments you would need to make (such as longer work hours, more regional travel, increased responsibilities and work stress, etc)? Are you prepared for this? Once you have resolved all these mental hurdles and are certain that this is a right move, go ahead and sign the offer letter without regrets or doubts.

Breaking the news to your boss

There are two outcomes that can arise from this: your boss will either take it well or badly, especially if this comes as a complete surprise. Some great bosses have congratulated their staff on landing better jobs with richer career prospects while others go to the other extreme of making things difficult for staff who leave. Some take such departures personally as an affront to their leadership style and feel rejected, while others may need staff to continue driving sales or close deals for them and are unhappy that their targets will not be met without him/her around.

When breaking the news of your resignation to your boss, remember the sole objective of the meeting is to notify your boss that you are tendering your resignation—you are neither asking for permission nor justifying the reasons for leaving.

You may be probed for your reasons for resignation but you are not obliged to elaborate. You are also not obliged to tell him which company you are joining, what role you are moving into or how much more the new job will pay you. Just let him know you are leaving the company and when your last working day will be. That is all.

Keep it professional. Highlight your planned timeline for handing over your current responsibilities to your colleagues. And never burn bridges, even if you are tempted to sneak a 'serves you right for treating me bad' look—you might work with him again soon or be required to furnish him as a character referee several jobs down the road.

BONUS MATERIAL

What does your boss's reaction to your resignation have in common with grief management? Visit www.career-strategy.com/bonus and key in "grief" to find out.

The counter-offer

Once you've delivered the bad news, your boss and HR may try to retain you in the form of a salary increase, a fancier title, a promotion or even the corner office with a view.

Now, even though it feels nice to be courted by your boss like this and the view from the corner office is really tempting, you need to consider some issues before you accept their counter offer.

Does your company really treasure your services or are they buying time to get a replacement?

The counter-offer often serves as a delay tactic for companies to stall you until a replacement can be found. Once you have signaled your intention to leave, you are a known flight-risk and a liability to their operations. The gears to getting your replacement will start moving. Because it takes roughly six months to get a new person on board, they still need you for now, hence the counter-offer. Many candidates naively fall prey to this tactic only to be fired six months down the road when their replacement arrives.

Why does the company only give you a raise when you threaten to resign?

Are they being sincere? Most counter-offers have been anywhere from a 10 percent to 20 percent increase in earnings. Even though this is enticing, why weren't you worth that much to them yesterday? Will you have to repeat the threat every time there is a salary review meeting for the rest of your career? What type of company do you work for if they only give you what you are worth when you threaten to resign?

How will you be perceived in the organisation if you accept the counter-offer?

Your bosses will still think of you as a flight-risk; your colleagues may paint you as an attention-seeker and your reputation (and personal pride) will take a blow because truth be told, you were bought. Accepting a counter-offer hints that you were not really looking for a job in the first place and was simply looking for a raise. Once the word gets out, the relationship that you now enjoy with your co-workers will never be the same. You will lose the personal satisfaction of peer group acceptance.

What is the real risk of accepting the counter-offer?

Anecdotal evidence suggests that those who do accept the counter-offer usually end up leaving the company within six months, either on their own accord or are replaced. What's the worst that could happen then (besides being unemployed)?

When it comes to that stage, you have effectively burnt your bridges with both your employer (you left them after you accepted the counter-offer) as well as the company which you turned down (you reneged on their Letter of Appointment). Both would hesitate to rehire you for a very long time. Given the speed at which news travels, your competitors' HR departments could learn of this and might even issue a 'do-not-hire' warning to their line managers against your profile.

REAL-LIFE CAREER STORY

Alfonso, R&D Director

Alfonso was the brains behind the company's operations. He had been the driving force for his Taiwan-based company's innovative products and was liked by his bosses, a husband and wife team who owned the business. They knew the company would not exist without him.

Alfonso had worked at the company for twelve years and even though he was underpaid, he was quite happy with his work. He wanted to have a share of the business but the owners always declined by saying, "We'll look into this next year."

He received a call from a headhunter one day and met with the other company out of curiosity. It was love at first sight for both parties and they offered him a hefty increment, his own research and development team to lead, as well as company stock.

With a signed letter of offer in hand, he came back to tender his resignation. His employers' first reaction was one of shock and then grief. The owner's wife cried in sorrow, saying how much she would miss him and his boss broke into tears and begged him not to leave, citing the long relationship they had and how he had always treated him like a son.

That evening, the owner, his wife, and their three children visited his home bearing gifts. The children were crying and begging poor Alfonso not to leave or they would be penniless. The owner's wife offered to double his salary. Being the nice guy he was, Alfonso agreed to the new terms and withdrew from the other offer, much to the chagrin of the headhunter and prospective employer.

The next few weeks, Alfonso was treated like royalty in his old company and felt really appreciated. Three months down the road, he was called into the owners' office. "I wonder what they are going to do for me now?" He pondered as he took a seat.

Both owners looked smug and told him he was fired. It had all been a stalling technique to buy time while they headhunted a replacement for him. Once the new guy signed on, Alfonso was unceremoniously let go.

In desperation, he called the headhunter but was told the job had already been filled. The headhunter refused to work with Alfonso anymore as he was a proven CRO (jargon for 'Candidate-Rejected-Offer') risk that no consultant would dare to present to their client again.

Do's and don'ts before you quit

It is rarely a nice experience telling your boss you are resigning and some of us even feel bad about it. Stick to these guidelines and you should be safe.

Do

* Keep your intentions confidential. Do not tell anyone—not even your best friend or colleague. Keep it private as it is preferable for your boss to hear this from you directly rather than through the office grapevine.
* Clear all the medical check-ups with the new company before tendering your resignation. Avoid a nightmare scenario where you are informed by your new company that a terminal disease was diagnosed during the check-up and the offer is being rescinded after tendering. You would then face the double-whammy of having no job and no medical coverage from either company.
* Develop a handover action plan for your team and boss for continuity after your departure so you don't burn any bridges.
* Prepare yourself for being walked out of the office. This happens when you are relieved of all duties with immediate effect upon tendering your resignation and are asked to leave the company's premises on the spot. You may be supervised by security as you clear your desk and may not even have time to bid your colleagues farewell. All items you remove may be inspected and anything deemed sensitive retained. You might want to remove all personal or sensitive information first (legally, of course) prior to tendering your resignation in anticipation of such a scenario.

Don't

- Don't remove or steal confidential data regarding client information, deal details, purchasing patterns, etc. Don't try to remove information through your USB thumbdrive or by emailing the data to yourself as it is extremely easy for the IT department to trace. Moreover, in some sectors (like banking) where secrecy laws are enforced, it could constitute a criminal act that might result in a trial and conviction.

- In the same vein, do not *delete* any work-related confidential information from your hard disk or go into a shredding-frenzy. If you need to shred anything, put it aside and clear it with your boss after you have tendered so no one can accuse you of destroying sensitive data.

- You should not remove name cards, training materials or Standard Operating Procedures (SOP) manuals as these can be construed as confidential information and removal of such materials could contravene your employment contract.

- Do not keep any personal information on your hard disk after your departure. This could be the innocuous family vacation photos, to the more incriminating type of data you collect while surfing the Internet during your free time—cover-letters for job applications to competitor firms and other stuff. You would probably want to delete personal spreadsheets involving your outstanding housing loans, bank balances and monthly family budgets.

> **BONUS MATERIAL**

To safely delete personal information from the company's hard drive, visit www.career-strategy.com/extra and key "safedelete".

Chapter 13

Handling your headhunter

My first encounter with the term "headhunter" was when I was an undergraduate. One mentor, a widely respected general manager with a US semiconductor company could not tolerate the office politics in his workplace after being chewed out by his unreasonable boss for the third time that week, so he walked up to his Managing Director and tendered his resignation on the spot. I recall his wife telling me how distraught he was at that time.

Shortly before lunchtime, he received a call from a headhunter who had heard from the grapevine that my mentor had quit that morning and wanted him to have lunch with the Managing Director of his biggest competitor. He went to that lunch meeting and by 4pm, had a signed offer letter in hand.

What manner of sorcery is that? My young and immature mind wondered. *Someday, I hope I'll be headhunted too!*

In 2004, I was.

When I first joined this exciting industry, I learnt that there are two types of search people—headhunters and recruiters.

Headhunters are executive search professionals who work mostly on senior-level roles for their clients. They are paid a retainer fee upfront for their service and progressive payments are made over the course of the search. This ensures that the consultant's time is purchased and he becomes a dedicated resource during the process, proactively searching for the right candidates. His *modus operandi* is not to advertise in the jobs-wanted advertisements of the papers or even online, as he targets the top performers who are not looking out for a job. Using his market knowledge, he methodically maps out the entire candidate pool and approaches each individual to assess him or her, then shortlists the top three to present to the client. This entire process can take up to two months—some CEO searches may even take up to twelve. In a nutshell, he is stalking his quarry and hunting with with a high precision sniper rifle.

Recruiters, on the other hand, tend to handle less senior roles and are often paid only when a successful placement occurs. Their clients often hand out assignments to multiple recruiters at a go, who will compete to grab any candidate they can find to present to the client. Because of the time constraint and high chance of not closing a deal, they usually adopt a shotgun approach to hunting and will place job advertisements to attract as many people as possible.

Both methods have their supporters and detractors. The different types of search methodologies will affect the candidates directly. Most executives prefer to be reached by headhunters as these professionals are able to spend more time talking to you and understand your career needs. They find the process a lot more relational rather than transactional.

What to do when a headhunter calls

When you receive a call from the headhunter, remember to ask these six important questions.

Question 1: Find out which company he is from

If you are unsure or the name is unfamiliar, do a quick search online for the firm—a peek into their corporate website will give you an indication of the size and branding of that firm. If he belongs to any of the better known ones, you are probably in safer hands. If his corporate website is a one-page write-up filled with typos, you should proceed with caution.

Question 2: Ask about the client

Sometimes, it could be a confidential search so he may not reveal who the client is. But try to get as many hints as you can from him. Such as how big is the company? Is it US or European? Are they a direct competitor? If the company is from your industry, you can probably guess who it is from how these questions are answered.

Question 3: Ask if it is a contingency or retained search

If it is a retained search, you can rest assured that you are talking to the right person with the authority to present a shortlist of suitable candidates to the client. Often, a contingency search means that even though you may be on his shortlist of three candidates, it could also mean that you may then be one of nine presented (including those presented by the other two recruiters fighting for the deal) to the client. Those are pretty bad odds.

Question 4: Find out more about the role

Is it a newly-created role or a replacement one? If it is the latter, what happened to the incumbent? Did he quit or was he fired? Why? What are the key challenges for this role? What is their organisation structure like? Is there a team reporting into it? Whom does this role report to? What are the KPIs? Ask for the job description document.

Question 5: Find out the client's salary range for the role

You may be too expensive or it may be too senior for you, so knowing this information upfront helps qualify the discussion so nobody's time is wasted.

Question 6: Ask him whether you are a good fit

Tell your career history and achievements, then ask whether it's a good fit for the position. Answer all questions truthfully.

Six things to do with the headhunter

1. *Always be polite.* Just like you, he has a job to do and you might just be the twentieth person he is calling that day, so do not give him a tough time. Even if the job is not relevant to you at this point in time, be nice so that he will remember you for future opportunities. I have had my fair share of

prospective candidates who rudely slammed the phone down on me. I usually don't call them again, even when a really exciting role comes up in the future.

2. *Begin a relationship.* If a headhunter asks you out for coffee, say yes even if you are not really interested. You'll gather useful information about salaries or about your industry and stay on his radar for other likely roles. Remember, it is always wise to build a relationship with a headhunter before and not when you need him.

3. *Be honest.* Share your ideas, thoughts, concerns, plans for the future, etc. Ask for advice. During your informal discussion, you could find out more about the market and seek his advice on your profile.

4. *Be helpful.* If he is not familiar with your industry or sector, give him ideas or advice of which companies he may want to target. Even better, refer friends who you think are suitable. Headhunters always like a good 'referrer' and will remember you for the help.

5. *Be open-minded.* Listen and ask questions. Do you feel that now isn't quite the best time to leave your company? You would be surprised how many of my successfully placed candidates weren't planning to leave their jobs when I contacted them for the role. Does the job sound too big and hairy for you? Often, the client may only have a general idea of how senior a newly-created role should be and even though the title may read 'Regional MD', at the heart of it, it could be only a sales director role. Ask for more time to think about it instead of declining upfront.

6. *Be professional.* Do not take it personally if the headhunter doesn't call back or feels you are not suitable for the role. We operate with a very strict set of search parameters and through

our questions, we will be able to get a feel of whether you are right for the role. You would probably not want to take on a job that isn't a good fit anyway, so trust his judgment. In such a situation, keep it cordial and follow up with him every six months, just to keep yourself on his horizon.

A friendly warning

As in all professions, there are always some who sully the good name of the industry as a whole. Headhunting is no different. Because the prize at stake is huge (search firms charge between 30 to 33 percent of the candidate's annual salary), the incentive for a small number of less scrupulous headhunters to misbehave is similarly large. Some recruiters will weasel a CV out of you for a non-existent job just so that they can slide your profile to their client (without your knowledge or consent), tagging your profile as 'theirs', in the event you do get hired. They will then claim a recruitment fee on your behalf. This practice hurts you because through no fault of yours, you have suddenly become 25 to 33 percent more expensive than the next candidate and that could hurt your chances of being hired.

Here are six warning signs to avoid getting stuck in such a situation with unscrupulous vendors:

1. *You have not heard of the company.* There are over 5,000 employment agencies in a tiny country like Singapore alone and each is licensed to carry out recruitment activities. Many are run by individual operators and all one needs to be a self-proclaimed headhunter today is a mobile phone and internet connection. If you haven't heard of the company, can't find it on the internet or if their corporate website looks unprofessional, be very cautious.

2. *He refuses to give any information regarding the client.* While we do conduct confidential searches from time to time, if the recruiter keeps giving very vague responses like "Our client is a Fortune 500 company in the IT industry" and nothing else, even refusing to specify what products or services, chances are high that this is a 'fishing' expedition with a non-existent job, designed to extract a CV out of you.

3. *He doesn't seem to know much about the role or doesn't want to answer questions.* In such situations, it could be that he doesn't know much about the role as he has not been fully briefed by the client. Would you buy a wrapped-up product without knowing what's inside? Such behaviour is highly suspicious. A professional headhunter will admit he doesn't have the information yet.

4. *He appears 'shifty' or unprofessional.* If you get the feeling that the recruiter is not being honest or is making up the answers to your questions as he goes along, be on your guard. At best, he could be a very young and inexperienced recruiter, or at worst, a dishonest one. Either way, you should proceed with caution, just in case.

5. *He thinks you are qualified and wants to shortlist you, but refuses to meet.* According the Association of Executive Search Consultants (AESC) guidelines, shortlisted candidates must be interviewed in person (or via skype) at least once. If the consultant says you made the shortlist yet doesn't even want to meet, something is terribly fishy.

6. *He keeps bugging you to send your CV, even though the role doesn't seem to fit or you are not interested.* Once again, this is a telltale sign of a CV-squatter—someone who would squat on your profile with as many companies as possible so that they can file a claim when you join the company.

In conclusion, it is always exciting and flattering to get a call from a headhunter. Your headhunter should be a primary source of information regarding the role and the client. He should be in full possession of important details like what the KPIs of the roles are, what expectations and immediate challenges the successful candidate faces, and even information like what the culture of the organisation is like, as well as the working style and temperament of the hiring manager (a good headhunter would have met the hiring manager at least once). If you know how to handle your headhunter, that would be the first step in the right direction for you.

BONUS MATERIAL

What are the four biggest blunders made by candidates during the headhunter's first call? Visit www.career-strategy.com/bonus and key "bigmistake".

Chapter 14

Help, I've been retrenched!

Shortly after the September 11 attack in 2001, a long queue formed outside the headquarters of a large local bank one morning. These people were not depositors demanding for their money but employees who had just been informed that they were being laid off. The worst part about this exercise wasn't that the retrenched staff were being notified at the entrance of the lobby of the bank and that they were not allowed to enter the building to retrieve their belongings. ("Your items will be dispatched to you," they were told.) The worst part was that this was done barely a week before Christmas.

Retrenchments are part of today's world. Sometimes you see it coming while at other times it blindsides you like a speeding truck. It can happen to anyone and will be a very nasty period of your career if it ever happened to you. Indeed, we are seeing it happen more often as we progress into the near future.

In the past, only the non-performers of the organisation got the pink slip—a way of 'cutting the fat' from the company. If your name was pulled out, you were most likely at the bottom of the staff-appraisal ranking. However, in today's hire-and-fire world, this is no longer the case. Shorter product life cycles, unreasonable targets promised to stockholders and even the vagaries of the marketplace often put real pressure on the company's bottom line and unfortunately, for many CEOs, the quickest way to improve profitability is to remove the biggest cost on the list—manpower. With the intense level of mergers and acquisitions too, large companies may fall prey to an even larger one, resulting in major re-organisation and retrenchments down the line.

So no job will offer an iron rice-bowl anymore. Top companies like Shell and Standard Chartered Bank used to have a lifetime employment policy in the sixties to eighties, but not anymore. Even public servants are constantly under pressure to perform.

It doesn't matter whether the role is being occupied by a top performer or that such talents are rare in the market—if it can be removed, it will be. It isn't personal. As such, even good staff are let go. In this connection, there is no longer a stigma to being retrenched or made redundant. What used to be a label of failure is now seen as part of modern working life.

This chapter will start by looking at the warning signsthat a retrenchment exercise may be heading your way so that you can be prepared to take action. We then explore your strategies for coping with being laid off—what to do and watch out for. It will conclude by examining the reasons why this happened and how you can move ahead with your career and life.

It is always good to be able to see the writing on the wall well in advance so that you can take pre-emptive action. If you can read the signs, you will be way ahead of the curve. Here are some indications that a layoff could be imminent.

Eight warning signs of retrenchment

1. *Your industry is struggling and other companies in your sector are retrenching.* During the Asian financial crisis in 1997, many industries in Asia were badly hit by the economic instability in the region and started to downsize. Across Asia, large companies, including the badly hit oil companies, also retrenched a significant number of staff. So if you see your competitors handing out pink slips, chances are that your company will be tempted to follow suit shortly. Be prepared with an exit strategy.

2. *Your company announces weaker earnings for several quarters in a row.* In today's context of stockholders demanding higher returns on their investments, many public-listed companies are forced to trade long-term strategies for short-term profits.

As such, the stock market can be extremely intolerant of any ebb and flow of earnings and will not hesitate to punish listed companies that are not performing. If your company has not been delivering on your CEO's promises, he may be pressed to cut costs and often, headcount is reduced. So watch out for those announcements.

3. *Changes at the top.* When your company has been acquired, there will probably be a layoff ahead. Belonging to the acquiring company does not guarantee your safety either, as you may also be asked to go. A change to the ownership is not the only event to watch out for. Sometimes, a new CEO or MD parachutes in with the aim of turning things around— and many times, the key doctrine behind this move is is a 'new broom sweeps clean' philosophy where he will make the necessary painful cuts to improve the bottom line.

4. *Headquarters engage overpriced efficiency experts to redefine the corporate mission or streamline operations.* Usually, these types of strategy sessions should be run by the local leadership team, but often, these external consultants are there to do the dirty work. So beware men in suits dashing around asking too many questions.

5. *When vacant roles aren't filled or when there is a total hiring freeze.* An early sign of tough times ahead is even at the expense of having one person doing the job of three, the company just can't justify the headcount. Such freezes are often initiated at the HQ level and is out of anyone's control.

6. *Your volume of work decreases significantly or you are increasingly left out of major projects.* If business is bad and you are sitting at your desk all day long waiting for projects, your job is in jeopardy. If this happens to you, it is clear that there is no need for your services. You are a sitting duck with a target on your back. Please start looking for new projects to do.

7. *When your company embarks on a series of extreme cost-cutting measures.* These could include no more drinking straws provided in the pantry or when the boss decides to move the entire team to a much smaller office in the boondocks where the rent is cheaper. They may even start to commence feasibility studies on whether your function could be outsourced to India. These are clear warning signs of the storm looming ahead.

8. *When HR or your boss asks if you can stomach a salary reduction or come in three days a week.* This is usually the final death knell before issuing you the pink slip. It is a cost-cutting measure that companies do in a last ditch attempt to rein in employment costs.

Truths of retrenchment

Now that you are aware of the warning signs, I would like to brace you mentally about this life-changing event will affect your life. Bear these truths in mind:

Truth #1: Retrenchment happens to the best of us and it just happened to you.

It is tough not to take it personally and feel rejected or embarrassed. But quickly get out of the downward spiral of unproductive self-pity. Your family needs you and you have to take action.

Truth #2: A new job search could take at least six to nine months.

This period gets longer the more senior you are. As the air is always much thinner at the top, senior job openings are fewer as well. Some people get a new role within a month—well, lucky them. With this time-frame in mind, plan your next moves around this period and remove any unrealistic expectations you may have.

Truth #3: *It is going to be stressful and demoralising.*

It will get worse before it gets better. Retrenchment comes with a whole bagful of negative emotions. I have observed that it hits men harder than women, possibly be due to the male-ego thinking that the man should always bring home the bacon. It is said that a man is defined by his work and losing his job will affect his confidence and self-worth. There will always be a period of mourning and adjustment, but if you discipline yourself and set the right moves in motion, things will look up after a while.

What to do if you are retrenched

There are four things you need to do as soon as you receive your retrenchment notice.

Negotiate for a fair separation package

While there is usually no iron-clad law on how much an employer has to pay a retrenched worker, companies are willing to be reasonable when letting staff go during a retrenchment exercise. Some large multinational companies give up to a month's salary for every year of service, but this amount varies.

Try to monetise as much of your benefits as possible—like un-utilised leave and even the termination notice-period. Try to negotiate for an ex-gratia payment, or even being allowed to stay on as a part-time consultant to oversee the transition period. Some companies may include an outplacement package where they will assign an outplacement firm to help you find a new job. Some executives find this useful but many feel that it is a waste of time and prefer to ask for the monetary equivalent of up to US$6,000) instead.

Be diligent and ensure that all money owed to you is promptly claimed and reimbursed in full. Items like entertainment or transport claims should be duly submitted and recorded for evidence. If you are in sales, walk through with your bosses and HR regarding the status of unpaid or future commissions and do not be afraid to be assertive about your rights.

Check your finances

Needless to say, you might be without a salary for the next six to nine months, or possibly, even a year. Do you have enough reserves to see you through this period? Do you need to make adjustments to your lifestyle and expenditures? Is there a need to liquidate assets to pay for the necessities?

Make a budget for the next nine months ahead, listing cash outflows, loan repayments, living expenses and other costs that you will be incurring. Review your cash position and take the necessary actions to make ends meet. To be entirely conservative, budget for a worst-case-scenario of an entire year of job-hunting and see if you have enough funds to see you through this upcoming drought.

Check your insurance

Many of us have never needed to worry about medical or hospitalisation costs because our employers have always provided corporate insurance. All we did was send the invoice to HR and the bills magically went away. Not anymore. Almost overnight, all insurance coverage for your family and you have evaporated and you are now fully liable for any accident, sickness or injury.

Review all your insurance policies for you and your family members and quickly purchase the minimum cover needed for a decent level of hospitalisation care for your loved ones and yourself. I have encountered an unfortunate situation where a friend was retrenched, and a month later, his wife got into an accident. Because he had no valid insurance, she had to stay in a C-class ward for over two months.

Inform your family

Having the breadwinner lose his job can be a very distressing situation for the family and out of the desire to protect our loved ones from undue worry, some retrenchees choose to keep this news away from their family. This is a bad move. You need to be open with your family as you will need their understanding and emotional support in the coming months. You will also have to plan how to make lifestyle changes and manage your expenses as a family. Take this as an opportunity to grow stronger as a family, and possibly, serve as an important lesson to your children on resilience in the face of difficulties.

What next?

After the shock of the retrenchment wears off, there are some constructive steps you need to take to rebuild your career and life. Take it as an opportunity to reflect on your career thus far and review which direction you would like your career to head towards. This period can be as tumultuous or as fulfilling a time you make it out to be.

Step 1: Review and reflect

You need to study the underlying reasons for your retrenchment. Was it due to a mass-retrenchment exercise over which you had no part to play or was it performance-based? If it was the latter, you need to find out what went wrong and avoid it in the next job.

However, if it was a mass-retrenchment exercise, was it company-specific (only your company downsized) or industry-specific (all your competitors also had to let people go)? If it is company-specific, why didn't your organisation do well? Was it their products, culture or management team? Uncover the reasons then try to look for a company without these characteristics so that the new one might face a better chance in the market you are in.

If the retrenchment is industry-wide, then you really need to reflect whether this is an industry you want to be in for the long haul or whether there is really no future in this sector anymore.

This thought process can be summarised as:

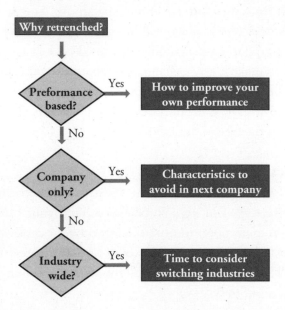

Step 2: Draw up a Career PLAN™
After you have assessed the reasons behind the retrenchment, draw up a Career Strategy (as elaborated in Chapter 3). Ensure that it is a robust one that leverages on your passions, strengths and market opportunities. Getting feedback from your mentor or career coach would be beneficial to ensure your plans are realistic and heading in the right direction.

Step 3: Kickstart a career search
With a PLAN in hand, embark on a career search plan (highlighted in Chapter 6).

Step 4: Retrain or retool

You might also want to consider whether your skillsets or knowledge have become obsolete. If you have mastery of a field or technology that has been outmoded, you run the risk of being redundant no matter which company you move to.

You may need to retrain and re-tool to make yourself more relevant to the job market. This may involve having to upgrade your skills via external courses or even getting under the wing of a mentor who will transfer his knowledge to you. We need to ditch the mentality that we might be too old to learn new skills, for we have to keep staying sharp and relevant in this knowledge-based economy.

Step 5: Talk to others

Keep talking to people. These could include your peers, your ex-bosses, and headhunters trawling your industry. Staying active in your social network will not only energise you but also allow you to be fresh in everyone's minds when the right job opportunity comes along. You do have more time on your hands now, so reconnecting with old buddies in the industry should be an enjoyable past-time.

REAL-LIFE CAREER STORY

Edgar, former Regional Supply Chain Director

Edgar spent fourteen years with his company and considered himself fairly lucky. At 46, he had four lovely daughters—Shirley 15, Sally 12, Sheryl 10 and Amy 7—and his wife was a stay-at-home-mom.

He was a regional supply chain director with a freight company that filed for bankruptcy during the financial crisis of 2009. He called me looking for a job. Because he sounded like a really nice family man, I agreed to meet and give him some career advice.

He shared that because the company was insolvent, there would not be any retrenchment benefits. He saw the writing on the wall a year ago when the company started reducing their fleet of vehicles but paid no heed to it, thinking that owners knew what they were doing. But he turned up to work one day in August and was locked out of the premises (together with his entire team) as the creditors seized the assets.

"My first reaction was one of shock as nobody had anticipated it. We were all confused and some were crying. I couldn't believe it was happening to me. It felt like a bad dream. I said to myself, 'This can't be true—not to me!' and started to feel angry. I was angry at the owners for not giving us advance warning. I was angry at myself for not reading the signs. I didn't know what to do. We demanded to speak to HR and when we did, we tried our best to get a deal out of them, but to no avail as even the HR Manager was caught unaware. I then started to feel afraid. What if I couldn't find a job? After all, I'm already 46. Would my family think of me as a failure now that I've lost my job? I knew I had enough savings to last a while, but what if I couldn't get a job that paid the same amount of money as before? Will my family need to downgrade? I took it pretty hard and stayed at home, being grouchy for three weeks before my wife told me to pull myself together for the kids. She said she trusted me and encouraged me to proactively look for a job."

That was when Edgar contacted me.

I walked Edgar through these tough times and even though he knew that I could not get him a job, he was happy to know that was not alone in feeling this way.

I advised him to look at the next six months as a career break and spend some quality time with his family (with his busy traveling schedule, he never saw his daughters very much) and enjoy their company.

Edgar took my advice and after four months, he managed to find a job that didn't pay as well as his previous one but was local-based, which meant that he got to see his girls more often. Sure, they had to cut back on their expenses, but as his youngest daughter Amy puts it, "It's still a great deal—we sacrifice a little but we get a whole lot more of Daddy!"

I asked him what advice he could share with others who might be going through this and he said, "Getting laid off is tough, but come to terms quickly and plan a strategy. Take it as an opportunity to refocus on your life, and enjoy the break while you can—if you keep up a positive attitude, you will land something good in no time."

In today's world, retrenchments are not always your fault so there is hardly any negative stigma associated with it anymore. You need to review and reflect on where things went off-track and take corrective action for the future.

Do keep your spirits high and stay in touch with your friends—you will ultimately get another job and when you do, you will look back at this challenging period and chuckle that it wasn't so bad after all,

BONUS MATERIAL

Ever wondered what you could do during your career break? Visit www.career-strategy.com/bonus and key "break" to access this extra article.

Conclusion

"A journey of a thousand miles begins with a single step."
—Lao Tzu, Chinese philosopher (604 bc–531 bc)

I am humbled that you have allowed me to share my thoughts and experiences with you. Your career is a forty-year journey that is filled with adventures, trials and rewards. Now that you have a deeper understanding of your Career Strategy, you are certainly better equipped for the road ahead. Do bear in mind these four important nuggets of wisdom.

Your career is *the* most important asset you own

Your career is the biggest asset and will generate monthly dividends (salary), so you must have a Career Strategy to make sure that it is kept on track. With the right Career Strategy, you will be able to *enhance* this asset and make it yield higher dividends in the long run, so begin to craft your Career Strategy today.

Your career is a marathon, not a sprint

Some candidates with top grades at Ivy League universities excel in the first ten years of their career, shooting up the corporate ladder only to burn-out before they hit 35, with still another thirty years of work left. But mentally exhausted, these high-fliers decide to drop out of the corporate world altogether. As

As mentioned earlier, your career is a forty-year journey. Always bear in mind that your career is a forty-year journey. Pace yourself well and you will find more enjoyment in your work and your success will be more sustainable.

Get a career mentor or career coach

You wouldn't mind spending money on upgrading your rental property to increase its rental yield, so why not invest in a career coach to enhance the biggest asset you own? Paying for a seasoned set of eyes to look for blind-spots in your Career Strategy could easily yield many multiples of what you put in.

Know your priorities

Life is like a juggling act. Imagine yourself struggling to keep three balls in the air—our career ball, our health ball and our family ball. Unfortunately, most of us have only two hands that have to constantly keep all three balls moving.

However, there is a fundamental difference between these three balls that we often don't realise until it is too late—the health and family ball are made of glass, whereas the career ball is made of rubber.

If there comes a time when the pressure of keeping all three balls in the air is so great that you have to select which one to let go, choose the career ball. It is made of rubber and will bounce right back up.

Because the family and health balls are made of glass, they will shatter when dropped and you may never be able to put it together again. If you are so focused on your career to the exclusion of your family and health, you might regret that decision. Life is far too precious so we need to prioritise what is important to us so that we can live a balanced and satisfying one.

I hope this book has been able to provide you some ideas on how to nurture an exciting and sustainable career. Do visit www. career-strategy.com for updates, interactive articles and news regarding career seminars, career clinics and career coaching packages. If you have any thoughts or feedback you would like to share, please email adrian@career-strategy.com.

Epilogue

When I conceptualised this book in 2009, I wondered whether it would ever get published. My first draft was completed but shelved when my father passed away that year. I felt that at the time, a 36-year-old headhunter had not 'earned his spurs' to give advice to senior business leaders much older than him.

In cold hibernation, the project was revived in early 2013 when I realised that today, more than ever, executives needed a career guide and framework to manage their careers. Hence, the original draft was thrown away and a new version was developed.

The journey I took to get this book published was an exciting one. However, as I was writing the book, giving advice on Career Strategies and monitoring market trends, I turned the lens to my own career and asked myself, "But Adrian, are you practising what you preach?"

Having spent almost a decade at Boyden Global Executive Search, was I being too comfortable? Was I turning away headhunter calls? (Yes, there is rampant poaching for top talents in the Executive Search industry too.)

Interestingly, I received a call from CTPartners, a US-listed top-tier executive search firm and had several great conversations with the leaders there. I had always respected that firm and was excited when they invited me to join their global team to handle their industrial clients in Asia.

So, after a decade in the same company, I am now with a dynamic new company, in a bigger role, and also in my discomfort zone (which is good). A mentor once told me that for each new role you move into, you need to be familiar with 60 percent of it; the other 30 percent has to be challenging and the remaining 10 percent terrifying. I think I understand now.

I am glad to have taken my own career advice and with your support, will continue monitoring the market and sharing great advice gleaned from my clients and candidates. See you online!

About the Author

Adrian Choo was born in Singapore and is a true seventies kid, growing up on a diet of Hanna-Barbera cartoons and listening to the Bee Gees and Johnny Cash on his dad's record player.

An entrepreneur at heart, he started a comics-trading business in school at the age of 16, and by 19, he started a company selling real human skeletons to medical students for study purposes. Nicknamed 'Bones', Adrian ran the business successfully until he graduated from Business School at the National University of Singapore with an Honours degree a semester before his peers. He then joined Shell as a Management Trainee where he imbibed the best practices of that much respected company.

In 2000, Adrian encountered his first career crossroad and left Shell to start a lifestyle marketing dotcom that lasted three years. He then joined a subsidiary of GE Plastics but deep down inside, he knew he hadn't fulfilled his calling. In 2004, he took an educated risk and followed his strengths and passion into the world of headhunting and has never looked back since.

As a seasoned headhunter with more than a decade of search experience behind him, Adrian has successfully placed CEOs and Senior Business Leaders of Fortune 500 companies including Shell, Samsung, Coca-Cola and many others. In this job, he plays the role of talent scout to his clients as well as career coach to his candidates—both roles he enjoys tremendously. Over the years, he has met, interviewed and made friends with hundreds of business leaders and has learnt a great deal about life from them.

Today, Adrian is a headhunter with CTPartners, a US-listed executive search firm with a sterling reputation and global track record. He handles the regional Industrial Practice from his base in Singapore. A loving father of two beautiful children, Lucius and Mia, he also volunteers his services as a board member of the Singapore Cancer Society, the country's oldest organisation dedicated to reducing the impact of cancer on patients and their families. His favourite activities include spending time with his family and collecting antique maps and curios.